Natural English:

The Conditionals Workbook

By Karolyn Close

ISBN-13: 978-1545456712

ISBN-10: 1545456712

1. Introduction

There are four conditional forms in English:

Zero Conditional

First Conditional

Second Conditional

Third Conditional

Each of them functions in a specific way under specific circumstances. Here is a quick introduction:

Zero Conditional is used for situations which we know to be generally true. It is often used for scientific observation but it can also be used for things you know about your own life. You can use words like **if, when, whenever, anytime, unless**. *(I'm allergic to strawberries. Whenever I eat strawberries I feel terrible.)*

First Conditional is used for normal, probable situations which are very likely to occur. Here you can use **"if"** or **"when"**. *(I'm going shopping. If I see a nice pair of shoes I'll buy them.)*

Zero and First Conditional are referred to as "real" conditionals. This means that they deal with real and normal situations in daily life.

Second Conditional is used for hypothetical, improbable situations or wishes. It is used for things which we understand are not very likely to happen. *(If I won the lottery I would buy you a new car.)*

Third Conditional is the only conditional used for situations which did or did not happen in the past. It is often used to express regret. *(If I had known you had problems I would have helped you.)*

Second and Third Conditionals are referred to as "unreal" Conditionals. This means that they are used for unreal situations, things that may never happen, or may or may not have happened in the past.

Zero Conditional	If/When + Present Simple + Present Simple	**If** I **eat** too much I **feel** sick.
First Conditional	If / When + Present Simple + Future Verb	**If** you **are** late I **will be** angry.
Second Conditional	If + Past Simple + Would + Infinitive	**If** I **saw** a UFO I **would run**.
Third Conditional	If + Past Perfect + Would have +Past Participle	**If** I **had seen** him I **would have reported** him to the police.

All conditionals are divided into two parts – 1) the *if clause* and 2) the *result / consequence*.

If one thing happens (or doesn't happen), there is a consequence.

Conditionals can also be expressed in this way:

There is a consequence if one thing happens (or doesn't happen).

It does not matter if the *if* clause goes first or second.

1.1 The use of "so" and "such"

Before we begin learning about Conditionals, we must take a look at the use of **so** and **such**. It may seem strange to include this in a workbook about Conditional forms but it is actually quite important.

So is an adverb. Though it's used in many different ways, we will only look at how it is used in a way similar to *very*, meaning *a lot*. The form is:

So + Adjective

She was **so happy**.	She was very happy.
They were **so lucky**.	They were very lucky.
That was **so interesting**.	That was very interesting.

Such is an adjective. It's also used to indicate *a lot* or *very*. **Such** goes together with an adjective and a noun. The form is:

*Singular = **Such** a / an + Adjective + Noun*

*Plural = **Such** + Adjective + Plural noun*

Singular noun	Plural noun
She was **such a happy girl**.	They were **such happy girls**.
That was **such an interesting story**.	Those were **such interesting stories**.

In order to use Conditional forms naturally in English, it is important to remember the correct use of **so** and **such**. Look at this statement:

My tooth is **very** painful. I can't sleep.

A non-native speaker of English might say: *Why is your tooth **very** painful?*

But the natural response for an English speaker would be: *Why is your tooth **so** painful?*

Here is a look at how **so** can function in Conditional sentences:

Zero Conditional (Imperative)	If your tooth is **so** painful, go to the dentist.
First Conditional	If you go to the dentist your tooth won't be **so** painful.
Second Conditional	If my tooth were **so** painful that I couldn't sleep I would go to the dentist.
Third Conditional	If you had gone to the dentist immediately your tooth wouldn't have been **so** painful.

Now look at this statement:

My boss is a **very** stupid man and I don't like working for him.

A non-native speaker of English might say: *Why is your boss a **very** stupid man?*

But the natural response for an English speaker would be: *Why is your boss **such** a stupid man?*

Here is a look at how **such** can function in Conditional sentences:

Zero Conditional	If your boss is such a stupid man then find a new job.
First Conditional	If your boss is such a stupid man you will be happier if you find a new job.
Second Conditional	If your boss weren't so stupid you would like your job more.
Third Conditional	If you had known your boss was such a stupid man you wouldn't have gone to work for him.

So and **such** both can mean "very" or "a lot" but we construct sentences differently when we use them:

So	*Such*
He is so stupid.	He is such a stupid man.
That soup is so delicious.	That is such delicious soup.
My cat is so fat.	She is such a fat cat.
That car is so expensive.	That is such an expensive car.
Today is so beautiful.	Today is such a beautiful day.

2. Zero Conditional

2.1 Forms

Zero Conditional is used for situations which are nearly always true or generally true. It is used to describe general truths, instructions, facts, habits and laws of science. Zero Conditional uses words such as **if, when** or **whenever, anytime, unless**.

One possible form for Zero Conditional is:

If/When/ Whenever + Present Simple Verb + Present Simple Verb.

Conditional sentences are divided into two parts: the condition part of the sentence (if) and the result or consequence.

Condition	Consequence / Result
If we **have** enough time on Fridays	we usually **watch** a film.
When I **forget** my keys at home	I **have to** call my brother to help me.

Examples

When the students **are** loud the teacher **gets** angry. (I know this happens because it happens every time.)

If I **forget** to call my mother she **gets** worried. *(I know this happens because in the past when I have forgotten to call, my mother is anxious.)*

Mary has terrible headaches. **If** she **drinks** red wine she **gets** a migraine headache. *(Every time Mary drinks red wine, she has a terrible headache. She knows this to be true.)*

I am allergic to pollen. In May, **when** there **is** a lot of pollen in the air, I **feel** terrible. *(It happens every spring.)*

When I **don't get** enough sleep I **am** tired and irritable. *(Every time I don't sleep enough, I am unpleasant all day long.)*

If you **rob** a bank you **go** to prison. *(This is the law and you know it to be true.)*

If you **don't have** money you **can't buy** a new car. *(No money, no car.)*

Whenever I travel I **like** to visit museums and churches. *(It's my usual habit.)*

2.1.1 Match the sentences:

a) If I don't sleep	I usually go with my friends.
b) When you talk very loudly	you give me a headache.
c) If I forget my umbrella	I am tired all day
d) If you are tired	I like to go shopping.
e) When the sun comes out	my dog hides under the bed.
f) If our cat is sick	go to bed.
g) If there is a good film playing on Fridays	it is quite warm.
h) If we have time during the summer	it rains.
i) When I have enough money	we usually take a long holiday.
j) If there is a big storm	we take him to the veterinarian.

2.1.2 Finish the following sentences from your own experience:

a) When it rains, I

b) When I have enough time, I like to

c) When I don't have enough time, I

d) If I don't sleep enough,

e) If a diabetic eats too much sugar,

f) When it is sunny, I

g) If she eats too much chocolate, she

h) When I eat too much I

i) If I forget my umbrella at home,

j) When I am late for work, my boss

k) If my dad works too late, my mother

l)   When the sun is shining I

m) If you leave ice cream in the sun,

n) When the sun comes out, the snow

o) When my alarm clock goes off in the morning,

2.1.3   You are asking Dr. Science-Guy a lot of questions. Fill in the gaps with Zero Conditional.

You: What happens when I put water in the freezer?

Dr. SG: When you _____ (put) water in the freezer it _____ (turn) to ice.

You: What happens when the sun goes down?

Dr. SG: When the sun _____ (go) down at night it _____ (get) dark.

You: What happens when I take ice out of the freezer?

Dr. SG: When you _____ (take) ice out of the freezer, it _____ (melt).

You: What happens when you add vinegar to baking soda?

Dr. SG: When you _____ (add) vinegar to baking soda, it _____ (make) carbon dioxide.

You: What happens when I drink a bottle of whiskey?

Dr. SG: When you _____ (drink) a lot of alcohol, you _____ (get) drunk and sick.

You: What happens in the spring?

Dr. SG: When the spring _____ (come) the weather _____ (turn) warm.

You: What happens in the autumn?

Dr. SG: When autumn _____ (come) the weather _____ (turn) cold and the leaves _____ (fall) off the trees.

You: What happens when you irritate your teacher?

Dr. SG: When you _____ (bother) your teacher, you _____ (get) into trouble.

You: What happens when people don't study for exams?

Dr. SG: When you _____ (not study) for an exam, you _____ (fail).

It is also possible to express Zero Conditional in this way:

Present Simple Verb + If/When + Present Simple Verb

Conditional sentences are divided into two parts: the condition part of the sentence (if) and the result or consequence. You can change their order in the sentence without changing the meaning.

Consequence / Result	Condition
We usually **watch** a film	**if** we **have** enough time on Fridays.
I **have to** call my brother to help me	**when** I **forget** my keys at home.

There is no difference in the meaning of these sentences. You can choose to put the *if* clause or the *consequence* clause first, whichever you prefer.

Examples

The teacher **gets** angry **when** the students **are** loud.

My mother **gets** worried **if** I **forget** to call her.

Mary has terrible headaches. She **gets** a migraine headache **if** she **drinks** red wine.

I am allergic to pollen. I **feel** terrible **if** there **is** a lot of pollen in the air.

I **am** tired and irritable **when** I **don't get** enough sleep.

You **go** to prison **if** you **rob** a bank.

You **can't buy** a new car if you **don't have** money.

I **like** to visit museums and churches **whenever** I travel.

2.1.4   Finish these sentences using Zero Conditional *if* clauses:

a)   I like to relax with friends if

b)   It usually rains if

c)   My best friend gets very angry if

d)   We always go for a walk in the park if

e)   I miss the bus in the mornings if

f)   We can't trust him if

g)   Danielle can't finish the project if

h) My boss takes us all out for lunch if

i) We see a play at the theatre if

j) Helen likes to eat lunch outside if

k) My grandparents love to cook big dinners if

l) Thomas gets a horrible stomach-ache if

m) I sleep late on Sundays if

n) They go on an expensive holiday if

o) We go swimming in the sea if

2.2   When/ Whenever /Unless

Zero Conditional can use **if** but it can also use **when, whenever** or **unless.**

If	If she has time she helps me with my homework.
When	When you leave your ice-cream in the sun, it melts.
Whenever (usually happens on many occasions)	Whenever I go out with my friends I have a great time.
Unless (if not)	Unless I wear sunscreen I get a horrible burn and I turn red.

If / when / whenever are used to indicate that something happens if a condition is met.

If I have enough money I take a taxi home from the theatre.
Whenever we talk about politics we have a terrible argument.
When I go shopping I stop for a coffee and a piece of cake.

Unless is similar to *if not*. It is used to describe what happens when a condition is not met.

Unless I take my medication, I go to the hospital.	If I don't take my medication I have to go to the hospital.
I can't sleep unless I have my favourite pillow.	I can't go to sleep if I don't have my favourite pillow.
You can't make a cake unless you have flour.	You can't make a cake if you don't have flour.

2.2.1   Fill in the blanks using if / when / whenever / unless

a) I don't think you can finish <u>unless</u>   I help you.

b) _____I get together with my old friends we usually talk about the past.

c) I don't like my aunt. She causes a problem _____ she comes to visit.

d) _____ you don't like your dinner, you don't have to eat it.

e) You pay a lot of money for a hotel _____ you get a discount.

f) Helen gets sick _____ she eats fish.

g) He acts like an idiot _____ he sees a pretty girl.

h) My dog gets scared _____ there's a thunder storm.

i) There's no possibility of skiing this winter _____ we get a lot of snow.

j) _____you want to improve you have to practice.

k) I can't help you _____ you don't tell me what the problem is.

l) Arthur shops like a crazy man _____ he has a little money in his pocket.

m) Water boils _____ it reaches 100°C.

n) The computer doesn't work _____ you don't plug it in.

o) The computer doesn't work _____ you plug it in.

p) _____ I don't drink coffee in the morning I'm a zombie all day.

2.3 Modal Verbs

Zero Conditional can also be expressed using modal verbs. Here is a table of modal verbs and how they function:

Permission / Request	Can	Can I go out with my friends this evening?
	Could	Could I use your pen?
	May	May I speak to you privately?
	Will	Will you help me?
	Would	Would you open the door for me?
Ability	Can	I can't swim at all.
	Could	When I was young I could sleep all afternoon.
Necessity / Obligation	Must	You must tell the truth.
	Have To	I have to study now. I have an exam tomorrow.
	Have Got To	I've got to go to the shops and buy bread and milk.
Prohibition	Mustn't	You mustn't make a lot of noise. The baby is sleeping.
	Can't	You can't park your car here. You'll get a ticket.
Advice	Should	You should go to sleep. You look tired.
	Ought To	I ought to call my grandmother and see if she's ok.
	Had Better	You had better do well on these exams or your parents will be angry.
Possibility	May	I may go out this evening if I finish all my work.
	Might	He might come over for coffee if he's free.
	Could	You should take a sweater. It could get cold later on today.
Probability	May	It may rain this evening.
	Might	We might go skiing if the weather is good.
Lack of necessity	Don't Have To	You don't have to eat the sandwich if you don't like it.
	Needn't /	You needn't be worried. Everything will be ok.
	Don't Need To	We don't need to be in a rush. We have a lot of time.
Preference	Would like	I'd like to have a coffee, please.
	Would prefer	I'd prefer to have a cup of tea.
	Would rather	I would rather not speak to her.

When a Zero Conditional sentence takes a modal verb, it can look like this:

If / When / Whenever + Modal Verb + Infinitive + Present Simple Verb	Present Simple Verb + If / When / Whenever + Modal Verb + Infinitive
When you **have to do** a lot of work it **is** best to make a plan.	It **is** best to make a plan **when** you **have to do** a lot of work.
If you **have pain** in your tooth you **should see** the dentist.	You **should see** the dentist **if** you **have** pain in your tooth.

It is also possible to use more than one modal verb in the sentence.

If / When / Whenever + Modal Verb + Infinitive + Modal Verb + Infinitive	Modal Verb + Infinitive+ If / When / Whenever + Modal Verb + Infinitive
If you **have to go** home now I **can stay** and continue working.	I **can stay** and continue working **if** you **have to** leave now.
If we **have to catch** the train at six o'clock we **should go** to bed early.	We **should go** to bed early **if** we **have to catch** the train at six o'clock.

2.3.1 Fill in the blanks with the correct modal verbs:

can't park, may visit, has to be, should work, had better leave, could finish must be, might be able, don't have to, can help, ought to clean, could explain, doesn't need to go, must take, would prefer to go,

a) If you _____ home we can leave now.

b) She _____harder if she wants the boss to promote her.

c) We _____now if we want to arrive in time for the film.

d) I _____to help you if you tell me what the problem is.

e) Henry _____more serious if he wants people to respect him.

f) If _____we finish this project today we might be able to go home early.

g) If you don't have a permit you _____your car here.

h) If you stop talking I _____the situation to you.

i) He _____ to work today. It's Sunday.

j) If you want to lose some weight you_____ more exercise.

k) We _____faster if you would help us.

l) We _____ the house if we're having company for dinner this evening.

m) I _____my friends tonight if I have time.

n) Shawn really _____ more organised if he is going to succeed.

o) Gerald _____me if I need any assistance.

2.4   If / Then

Zero Conditional sentences often use **if** and **then**. The **if clause** describes the condition and the **then clause** describes the result or consequence.

When the **if clause** is first in the sentence, you can use **then**. When the **if clause** is second in the sentence, you don't need to use **then**.

If clause comes first (then)	*If clause* comes second (no then)
If + Present Simple verb + then + Present Simple verb.	Present Simple verb + if + Present Simple verb
If the weather **is** good t**hen I go** for a walk.	I **go** for a walk **if** the weather **is** good.
If we **have** enough money **then** we usually **go** for a nice dinner.	We usually **go** for a nice dinner **if** we **have** enough money.
If I **don't sleep** enough **then** I **feel** horrible all day.	I **feel** horrible all day **if** I **don't sleep** enough.

2.4.1   Match the If and Then clauses to make complete sentences.

a) If we are free in the evenings	then he can buy a new car.
b) If you drink too much	then the boss gets angry.
c) If you watch too much television	then you get cavities.
d) If the baby makes a mess	then you need to take a jacket.
e) If I have a lot of work to do	then she embarrasses herself by shouting.
f) If Julia gets angry	then I have to go to hospital.
g) I'm allergic to fish. If I eat fish	then you will get a stomach-ache.
h) If the birds are singing very loudly in the morning	then we like to go out with our friends.
i) If Gabriel has enough money	then I make a list to help myself get organised.

j) It's cold outside. If you want to go for a walk	then then I clean it up.
k) If Maria gets a headache	then she takes an aspirin.
l) If you eat all that ice-cream	then I can't sleep.
m) If you practice piano every day	then you improve.
n) If you don't brush your teeth	then you get a headache.
o) If Polly leaves work early	then you get drunk.

If / then clauses can also take modal verbs.

If clause comes first (then)	*If clause* comes second (no then)
If you **have** an exam tomorrow **then** you **had better study**.	You **had better study if** you **have** an exam tomorrow.
If you still **have** a headache **then** you **should see** a doctor.	You **should see** a doctor **if** you still **have** a headache.
If you **don't have to do** any homework **then** we **could go** out tonight.	We **could go** out tonight **if** you **don't have to do** any homework.

2.4.2   Finish the sentences using modal verbs.

a)   If David wants to go to Tokyo then

b)   If we want to be on time for our class then

c)   If you don't want to get sick then

d)   If Layla wants to lose a few kilos then

e)   If Paul needs money then

f)   If you want people to respect you then

g)   If we don't have any homework tonight then

h)   If you don't know what to do then

i)   If you want to improve your English then

j)   If you feel sick then

k)   If he wants to finish this project on time then

l)   If Jack wants to catch the train at six o'clock tomorrow morning then

m) If we have time then

n)   If Mark takes the time to cook a lovely dinner then

o)   If Frances is interested in art then

2.5   Imperatives

An imperative is a command telling a person or people to do something. Forming the Imperative in English is very simple. You simply use the infinitive of the verb or the infinitive plus **don't**.

Command someone to do something	*Command someone **not** to do something*
Sit down.	Don't sit down.
Eat your vegetables.	Don't eat your vegetables.
Tell the truth.	Don't tell the truth.
Go home.	Don't go home.

Using the infinitive is not very polite. You can make it more polite buy saying **please** either at the beginning or the end of a sentence.

Please sit down.	Sit down, please.
Please eat your vegetables.	Eat your vegetables, please.
Please tell the truth.	Tell the truth, please.
Please go home.	Go home, please.

Zero Conditional often takes the Imperative.

If you want to go, go.	If you don't want to go, don't go.
If you need better grades in school, study.	If you need better grades in school, don't be lazy.
If you are sick, take your medicine.	If you're not sick, don't take medicine.
If you're hungry, eat.	If you're not hungry, don't eat.

Note that this is very similar to **if/then**.

If you want to go, **then** go.	If you don't want to go, **then** don't go.
If you need better grades in school, **then** study.	If you need better grades in school, **then** don't be lazy.
If you are sick, **then** take your medicine.	If you're not sick, **then** don't take medicine.
If you're hungry, **then** eat.	If you're not hungry, **then** don't eat.

2.5.1 **Delores is not happy about her life. Answer all her statements using Zero Conditional and the Imperative:**

a) My tooth hurts.   If your tooth hurts, (then) go to the dentist.

b) I'm tired.

c) I'm fat.

d) My hair is too long.

e) My fingernails are in terrible condition.

f) My flat is a terrible mess.

g) My stomach hurts.

h) My grades in school aren't very good.

i) I have no friends.

j) I'm a terrible dancer.

k) I'm hungry.

l) My clothes are dirty.

m) I have no money.

n) I have a lot of work to do.

o) I'm late for work.

p) My car broke down last night.

The Imperative with 'you'

Sometimes when we use the Imperative with the pronoun **you**, we don't mean the person we are speaking to, but speaking about what people in general should do. This is often used to give advice or our opinions about how life should be.

If you want to keep fit you need to exercise every day.	I'm not speaking to you, in particular. I'm talking about what people should generally do.
If you want to save some money you have to plan more carefully.	This is true for all people, not just the person I am speaking to.
If you want a friend you have to be a friend.	I don't necessarily mean you, the person I'm speaking to. I mean that this is generally true for all people.

2.5.2   Here are some problems. Give some general advice about life using you and the Imperative.

a)   Finding friends   If you want to find friends you have to go out and meet people.

b)   Having a lot of stress

c)   Being more organised

d)   Staying physically fit

e)   Being more relaxed

f)   Having more free time

g)   Dealing with difficult people

h)   Feeling tired and with no energy

i)   Not having enough money

j)   Finding love

k)   Being unhappy with your life

l)   Having problems at work

m)   Feeling sick all the time

n)   Not knowing how to cook good food

o)   Don't know where the best places to shop are

p)   Looking for something interesting to do

2.6   Zero Conditional with Present Continuous

Zero Conditional can also be used with Present Continuous. The form is:

If / Whenever / Unless + Present Continuous +Present Simple

Often, the sentence is reversed so the Present Simple verb comes first. (It sounds more natural this way)

Present Simple + If / Whenever / Unless + Present Continuous

I don't answer the phone if I'm working.
Phil interrupts us whenever we're talking.
She doesn't like to go out unless she's wearing full make-up.

Zero Conditional with Present Continuous is often used with modal verbs or imperatives to explain habits or rules.

Zero Conditional with Modal Verb	Zero Conditional with Imperatives.
You mustn't talk to me when I'm driving.	Don't bother me when I'm driving.

2.6.1   Match up these sentences.

a) Don't talk to me	if it's raining.
b) My father gets angry if I wake him up	unless I'm going to a party.
c) Hilary never wears her glasses	if Randall made it.
d) I never wear elegant clothes	if you're speaking so quietly
e) Joseph sends me a postcard	when he's sleeping.
f) They are never happy	unless she's driving her car.
g) I won't speak to her about important things	if you're feeling sick.
h) Pamela can't hear you.	then make yourself a sandwich.
i) I'm not drinking that coffee	if she is drinking.

j) Melissa stays up late every night	whenever he is travelling.
k) I prefer not to answer the phone	unless they are working.
l) Close the windows	if it's ringing.
m) If you're feeling hungry	when I'm working.
n) Go to the doctor	when I'm talking on the phone
o) Answer the phone	unless she's feeling tired.

2.7   Zero Conditional Sample Texts

Here are some sample texts to demonstrate how Zero Conditional works. Underline the Zero Conditional sentences.

a) Martha is coming over to my house tonight. Whenever we are together we have a good time. If the weather is good we often go eat dinner outside on the terrace. If the weather isn't good we stay inside and watch movies or chat. Martha and I have very different opinions about life and sometimes we don't agree. If we don't agree we sometimes argue but we never stay angry for long. I think it's nice to have friends who don't share your opinions because then you can learn something new. If you only have friends who think like you do, you never learn anything.

a) My brother Ted is a disaster. He always gets into trouble at work, he never has any money and he's always calling our parents to help him out. If he calls my mother she runs to help him. If he calls my father, he doesn't get any help because my father gets irritated and angry with him. Naturally, when Ted is in trouble he doesn't call my father very often. I feel frustrated with Ted. If I tell him no and don't help him, he makes me feel guilty. Whenever he does something stupid we all have to rescue him. Last year he got arrested for breaking a shop window because he was mad at the owner of the shop. My father paid for that. This month I paid his rent. If we would stop helping Ted I believe he would have to learn how to be a responsible adult.

b) Unless I'm working I prefer not to check my email. I find that technology has taken over our lives to the point where we can't function unless we are looking at our email constantly. I hate it whenever I'm with a friend and she's always checking her phone for messages. I feel like I'm talking to myself. I think we have lost the ability to talk to each other directly. I think human contact is more important than virtual contact. In fact, at the weekends I don't even check my messages unless I absolutely have to. I prefer to read books, visit friends, go for walks or just relax. If I have my phone with me I feel like I always need to check it to see if I have a message. I'm always wondering if someone has written me or if I need to respond to anything. If you're always checking your phone for messages you can't really relax.

c) There are many things you can do if you have a lot of stress. Whenever you feel anxious or nervous you can do some deep breathing exercises. If you slow your breathing down you feel better. If you make a list of all the things that worry you then you can think about them logically and decide what to do. Whenever I'm feeling stressed or nervous I like to listen to music. My friend Matthew likes to clean his flat when he feels anxious. He says that if he cleans his house he always feels better and less stressed afterwards. My neighbour Janet says that if she's feeling anxious she likes to go for a run. Exercise helps relax and energise us whenever we feel unhappy or nervous. Stress is a part of life but we can always find ways to manage it.

3. First Conditional

3.1   Forms

First Conditional is used for situations which are very likely and probable. It is used for things that happen, or can happen every day.

The form for First Conditional is:

If / When + present verb + future verb (usually "will")

Conditional sentences are divided into two parts: the condition part of the sentence – if - and the result or consequence (**will / going to**).

if – the condition that must be met	*will/going to* – the result or consequence
If I see him	I will talk to him.
If we don't hurry	we will be late.

Incorrect: When I ~~will~~ have enough money, I will buy a car.
Correct: When I have enough money I will buy a car

There is always only one "will" per sentence!

When I **see** John I **will tell** him hello.	*It is quite normal for me to see him, and when I do see him, I will talk to him.*
I'm going shopping tomorrow. **If I see** something I like, **I'll buy** it.	*I will buy something only if I see something I like.*
We'll go to the cinema **if** we **have** enough time.	*If we don't have enough time, we won't go to the cinema.*
If I **have** enough money, **I'll buy** a car.	*If I don't have enough money, it won't be possible for me to buy a car.*
If you **don't study** for that exam, **you won't pass** it.	*To pass the exam, you must first study. No studying, no passing.*
If you **eat** all that chocolate, **you'll be** sick.	*If you don't eat all the chocolate, you won't feel sick.*

3.1.1 Match the sentences

a) If you don't understand the homework	we'll go to Morocco on our holiday.
b) If Jack hears this story	you will be successful.
c) If you make coffee for yourself	he will be very surprised.
d) If it rains	I'll drink some too.
e) If you work hard	I'll help you.
f) If she continues to come to work late	we will be late for our meeting.
g) If we don't hurry up	I will find someone else who can.
h) If you can't help me	we'll go on a picnic tomorrow.
i) If I have nothing to do this evening	we won't be able to go to the seaside.
j) If we see something nice in the shops	he will be very angry.
k) If the weather is good	I'll be very angry with you.
l) If we can find a cheap flight	we'll buy it.
m) If there's a good film playing	we'll go to the cinema tomorrow.
n) If you don't stop talking	the boss will fire her.
o) If he thinks he can do whatever he wants with no consequences.	I'll watch TV.

3.1.2 Finish the following sentences using First Conditional:

a) I'd like to go on a picnic today but if it rains,

b) I can see that you are having difficulty with Maths. I'm very good at Maths. If I have time,

c) If you drink ten beers,

d) I'm very angry at him. When I see him,

e) If you call me again,

f)   I can see you are angry with John. When I see him, I

g)   If we don't have any bottled water,

h)   If we go out for dinner,

i)   If I have enough money,

j)   If they call us to go out with them,

k)   When I finish school,

l)   If you don't tell me the truth,

m) When he calls me,

n)   My boss is away for a week and every day I have taken a very long lunch break. When my boss comes back,

o)   If I forget my umbrella,

3.1.3 You are having a conversation with Mr. Fickle. Lucky you! Fill in the gap with First Conditional:

Mr. F: I would like to go to the cinema today.

You: Oh, that's nice. What would you like to see?

Mr. F: Well, that depends. If they have an adventure film I_____ (not go) because I hate adventure films.

You: Oh. I see.

Mr. F: And if there is a romantic film I _____ (definitely not go) because I can't stand romantic films. I think they're awful.

You: Oh.

Mr. F: But if there _____(be) a thriller, I _____(go) because I like thrillers.

You: Oh.

Mr. F: But if the thriller is starring Peter Wonderful, I _____(not go) because I don't like Peter Wonderful. He's a terrible actor.

You: Oh.

Mr. F: But if there is a thriller, and that thriller doesn't have Peter Wonderful, I

_____(certainly go). Unless the popcorn is cold. If the popcorn _____ (be cold) I

_____ (not go). I hate cold popcorn.

You: Oh.

Mr. F: And also the price of the tickets is very important. If ticket _____(be too) expensive,

I _____(not go). Then again, if the ticket _____(not be) very expensive, I

_____(not go) because it probably means the cinema is old.

You: Oh.

Mr. F: I don't like old cinemas. If the cinema _____(be too old) , I_____ (not go). Then again,

I don't like it if a cinema is new.

You: Oh?

Mr. F: If the cinema _____ (be new) it _____(be) too busy and I don't like a cinema

with a lot of people.

You: Oh.

Mr. F: Well, I should go now. Thanks for the chat.

You: Oh. ☹

In the same way that it is possible to reverse the order of a Zero Conditional sentence, it is also possible to express **First Conditional** like this:

Will + Infinitive + If / When + Present Verb

will– the result or consequence	**If / when** – the condition that must be met
I will talk to him	if I see him.
We will be late	if we don't hurry.

Remember! We use <u>one will only</u>! Never two!

Not: If I̶ ̶w̶i̶l̶l̶ study I will do well on the exam.

Correct: if I study I will do well on the exam.

Examples:

I **will tell** John hello **when I see** him.

I'm going shopping tomorrow. **I'll buy** something I like **if I see** it.

We'll go to the cinema **If** we **have** enough time.

I'll buy a car **if** I **have** enough money.

You won't pass the exam **if** you **don't study** for it.

You'll be sick **if** you **eat** all that chocolate.

3.1.4 Finish the sentences

a) I won't speak to you if *you are rude to me.*

b) She will be very happy when

c) My grandmother will come and visit us if

d) I'll go for a pizza with my friends if

e) We'll watch a movie later if

f) I'll cook dinner if

g) Harry will clean the house if

h) I'll buy you a new sweater if

i) Kate will call you when

j)   They won't be happy when

k)   Gavin will go to Paris if

l)   Polly won't wear those shoes if

m)   We won't go skiing this winter if

n)   David will be late coming home this evening if

o)   Rachel will do the shopping if

p)   James will go to university if

3.2 When / As Soon As / Unless

First Conditional can be expressed using **if** but it can also take **when / as soon as / unless.**

If	If I have time I will help you. (This depends on if I have time.)
When	When I have time I will help you. (This will happen when I have time.)
As soon as (the first possible moment)	As soon as I have time I will help you. (At the first possible moment I will help you.)
Unless (if not)	I will help you unless I don't have time. (Not enough time, no help.)

If and **when** are used when something will happen if a condition is met.

If I drink coffee now I won't sleep tonight.	Drinking coffee will keep me awake. If I don't drink coffee, I won't stay awake.
When I finish correcting your homework I'll call you.	First I must finish correcting your homework and then I will call you.

As soon as is used to say something will happen at the first possible moment.

As soon as I hear from Robert I will send you a message.	The moment I hear from him I will tell you.
As soon as I get home I'll take a shower.	The moment I get home I will take a shower.
As soon as Angela sees this mess she will be furious.	Angela will be very angry the moment she sees the mess.

Unless is used to mean "if not"

I won't help you unless you tell me the truth.	I won't help you if you don't tell me the truth.
She won't eat anything unless it has a lot of salt.	She won't eat anything if it doesn't have a lot of salt.
You won't get fit unless you get some exercise.	You won't get fit if you don't do some exercise.

3.2.1 Fill in the blanks with if / when / as soon as / unless

a) We won't have fun at the party _____unless_____ Peter comes too.

b) Edward will tell us the story _____ he comes home.

c) Sam will be very happy _____ he hears the good news.

d) _____ she has enough money in her budget our boss will take us out for an expensive lunch.

e) I will be very angry _____ she's rude to me again.

f) _____ the situation improves we will have to find a new apartment.

g) Clean your room _____ you can.

h) I think I will improve my French _____ I practice a lot.

i) I will be very angry _____ you tell anyone.

j) I won't be able to do my report _____ the computer doesn't work.

k) They will call us from the airport _____ their plane lands in London.

l) My dog won't go outside _____ I go out with him.

m) You will get very sick _____ you stop smoking.

n) I won't go to the doctor _____ I feel very sick.

o) They'll buy a new house _____ they save the money.

p) William won't talk about his problems _____ you ask him directly.

3.3   First Conditional with Going To

First Conditional can also be expressed with **going to** instead of **will**. **Going to** can be seen as a stronger intention than **will**.

If I see her I'll talk to her.	*I promise / intend to speak to her.*
If I see her I'm going to talk to her.	*I absolutely intend to speak to her.*

3.3.1   Match the sentences

a) When she discovers what you've done	as soon as I save enough money.
b) William is going to be exhausted.	if you behave so badly.
c) I'm not going to speak with you again	if you continue to waste time doing stupid things.
d) You're going to be sick	unless they have the money.
e) I'm going to buy a new tablet	they're going to be very angry.
f) When Mum and Dad see this mess	she is going to kill you.
g) They're not going to buy a house	as soon as she gets home.
h) I'm going to visit Grandmother	unless he apologises for his rudeness.
i) Gina is going to start dancing again	as soon as you stop interrupting me.
j) Anna isn't going to invite him to her party	unless you plug it into the electrical socket.
k) I'm going to finish reading this book	if she's feeling better.
l) You're not going to be on time for work	I'm going to make you a lovely breakfast.
m) The television isn't going to work	when her leg feels better.
n) If I have time this morning	if you drink all that vodka.
o) Lana is going to call her parents	if he continues to work so hard.

3.4   If / Then

First Conditional can use **if/then**, each in a different part of the clause. **Then** goes with the consequence part of the clause (the **will / going to** part).

If	Then
If you go to Paris	**then** you'll see the Eiffel Tower.
If we don't get home on time	**then** Mum and Dad are going to be angry with us.
If Susan buys the pizza	**then** we'll buy the drinks.

3.4.1   Finish these sentences using your imagination

a)   If we get to the restaurant before it closes then *we will order dinner.*

b)   If you forgot your keys in the car then

c)   If the library is open then

d)   If the exam is on Tuesday then

e)   If you're tired then

f)   It's Sunday and we have time to relax. If you feel like it then

g)   If our neighbour has another loud party tonight then

h)   If you don't have time to wash the dishes then

i)   If Diana doesn't want to come to our party then

j)   If it's hot again tomorrow then

k)   If Jack keeps complaining about stupid things then

l)   If Theo isn't more polite to me then

m)   If Polly doesn't give me back the money I lent her then

n)   It's very cold today. If you wear that light summer dress then

o)   Let's clean the house together. If you wash the floors then

p)   If I get to the post office before it closes then

3.5   Modal Verbs

First Conditional can also take Modal Verbs. Here is a table of Modal Verbs and how they function.

Permission / Request	Can	Can I go out with my friends this evening?
	Could	Could I use your pen?
	May	May I speak to you privately?
	Will	Will you help me?
	Would	Would you open the door for me?
Ability	Can	I can't swim at all.
	Could	When I was young I could sleep all afternoon.
Necessity / Obligation	Must	You must tell the truth.
	Have To	I have to study now. I have an exam tomorrow.
	Have Got To	I've got to go to the shops and buy bread and milk.
Prohibition	Mustn't	You mustn't make a lot of noise. The baby is sleeping.
	Can't	You can't park your car here. You'll get a ticket.
Advice	Should	You should go to sleep. You look tired.
	Ought To	I ought to call my grandmother and see if she's ok.
	Had Better	You had better do well on these exams or your parents will be angry.
Possibility	May	I may go out this evening if I finish all my work.
	Might	He might come over for coffee if he's free.
	Could	You should take a sweater. It could get cold later on today.
Probability	May	It may rain this evening.
	Might	We might go skiing if the weather is good.
Lack of necessity	Don't Have To	You don't have to eat the sandwich if you don't like it.
	Needn't /	You needn't be worried. Everything will be ok.
	Don't Need To	We don't need to be in a rush. We have a lot of time.
Preference	Would like	I'd like to have a coffee, please.
	Would prefer	I'd prefer to have a cup of tea.
	Would rather	I would rather not speak to her.

When a **First Conditional** sentence takes a **Modal Verb**, it can look like this:

If / When / As Soon As / Unless + Modal Verb + Infinitive + Will / Going to	Will / Going To + If /When/ As soon as / Unless + Modal Verb + Infinitive
If you **have to stay** late tonight, **I will wait** for you.	I **will wait** for you **if** you **have to stay** late tonight.
If Mum **can drive** you to school now **I will pick** you **up** at the end of the day.	I **will pick** you **up** after school **if** Mum **can drive** you now.
If you **need to go** home **we will finish** the report by ourselves.	We **will finish** the report ourselves **if** you **need to go** home.

Often a **First Conditional** sentence with a Modal Verb does not have **If / When**. Instead it uses **Or**. In this case, there is no flexibility in how to arrange the sentence. The **Modal Verb** part comes first and **Or** comes second.

Modal Verb + Infinitive + or + Will / Going to + Infinitive	
We **should leave** now **or we're going to** be late.	I really **must go or I'm going to be** late for work.
I **ought to call** my husband **or** he **will be** worried about me.	You **have to study or** the teacher **will be** angry.

3.5.1   Fill in the blanks with the correct modal verbs:

can't help me can talk, had better tell, ought to prepare, could carry, must be, have to go, should do, must take, must study, had better go, ought to walk, have to go, don't have to go, should eat, has to

a) If you ___*can't help me*___ I'll call someone else.

b) I have a lot of time. I'll tell you when I_____.

c) I really _____ if I'm going to pass that exam.

d) You _____to the post office now or you won't be able to pick up your mail.

e) Ryan _____more responsible or his boss won't give him the promotion.

f) I _____the dog now or he'll start to whine and bark.

g) I _____the laundry or we won't have any clean clothes to wear.

h) As soon as I _____for a few minutes I will phone you.

i) If you _____the ten o'clock train you'll have to leave now.

j) If you _____to work today then I'll stay home too.

k) If you _____ the books then I'll carry the clothes.

l) Unless you _____ right now I'll start cooking dinner.

m) You _____me the truth or I'm going to be very upset with you.

n) You _____ now or you'll be very hungry later on.

o) We _____our picnic or we won't have anything to eat.

p) She _____ apologise or Jane won't forgive her.

3.6   Imperatives

An imperative is a command telling a person or people to do something. Forming the Imperative in English is very simple. You simply use the infinitive of the verb or the infinitive plus **don't.**

Command someone to do something	Command someone not to do something
Sit down.	Don't sit down.
Eat your vegetables.	Don't eat your vegetables.
Tell the truth.	Don't tell the truth.
Go home.	Don't go home.

Using the Imperative is not very polite. You can make it more polite buy saying **please** either at the beginning or the end of a sentence.

Please sit down. / Sit down, please.

Please eat your vegetables. / Eat your vegetables, please.

Please tell the truth. / Tell the truth, please.

Please go home. / Go home, please.

First Conditional can take the Imperative. Often the Imperative is in the Conditional part of the clause and **will / going to** is in the result part of the clause. We can use **and / or** in the sentences. **Or** usually indicates that there will be an unpleasant consequence.

And	Or
Sit down and we'll talk.	Sit down or I'll get upset.
Turn on the TV and I'll get the popcorn.	Turn off the TV and go to bed or you'll be tired tomorrow.
Wash the windows and I'll wash the floors	Wash the windows or I'll have to do everything myself.
Don't do your homework and you'll face the consequences.	Don't be lazy or you'll face the consequences.
Don't call Henry and tell him the news and he'll be disappointed in you.	Don't call Henry and talk about your problem or you'll be very upset.
Don't eat ice-cream before dinner and you'll lose weight faster.	Don't eat sweets before dinner or you won't be hungry later.

3.6.1   Finish the sentences using First Conditional:

a) Sit down or ___I'll get angry_____

b) Sit down and

c) Tell the truth or

d) Tell the truth and

e) Come here or

f) Drink your juice and

g) Don't be stupid or

h) Finish your homework and

i) Finish your homework or

j) Go to bed or

k) Don't make a mess in here or

l) We're going on a trip. Go put petrol in the car and

m) Make lunch and

n) Pack the picnic food and

o) It's raining. Close the windows or

p) Don't jump on the furniture or

3.7 First Conditional with Present Continuous

First Conditional doesn't just use **will / going to**. It can also take Present Continuous. We use Present Continuous in the conditional part of the clause to indicate a continuous / future action which may or may not result in the consequence part of the clause. The consequence part of the clause takes will / going to. The form is:

If + Present Continuous + will / going to

Condition - IF (Present Continuous)	Result / Consequence - (Will / Going to)
If you're having another beer	I'll have one too.
If we're eating out tonight	I'm not going to have a snack now.
If Mum is busy working	we won't disturb her.

3.7.1 Finish the sentences

a) If the baby is finally sleeping we won't make any noise

b) If the dog is jumping around at the door

c) If you're making more coffee

d) If she's cleaning the house

e) If Annie is cooking

f) If Tom is working tomorrow

g) If the teacher is getting angry

h) If you're having lunch

i) If you're driving your car to work today

j) If he's losing all his money at the casinos

k) If there's anything good playing at the cinema

l) If it's raining today

m) If Oliver is playing football tonight

n) If Edward is being disrespectful

o) If Daniel is taking a shower now

p) If the weather is getting colder

3.8   First Conditional with Present Perfect

First Conditional can also take Present Perfect, and you will often see **by / by then** in the conditional part of the sentence to indicate that something will happen no later than a certain moment. The form is:

If + Present Perfect + (by / by then) + will / going to

By is used with a specific time / date. **By then** is used when we already understand what that specific time / date is.

By*	By then
Please be home **by** ten o'clock or Mum will be angry.	Please be home **by then**. (We already understand that it's ten o'clock)
I think I'll be finished **by** Tuesday, at the latest.	I think I'll be finished **by then**. (We already understand that we're talking about Tuesday)

* Don't confuse **by** and **until**!

by = no later than a certain moment.
until = do something continuously and then stop at a certain moment.

> I arrive at work **by** eight o'clock every morning. (I arrive no later than eight o'clock.)
> I work **until** five and then I go home. (I work and work and work and at five o'clock I leave.)

Condition IF / Present Perfect	Consequence Will / Going to
If you **have finished** your work **by** four o'clock	the boss **will be** happy.
If you **haven't finished** your work **by then**	the boss **will be** very angry.
If she **has packed** her bag	we'll leave.

3.8.1 Match the sentences

a) Freddy will be hungry	I won't be able to send this stupid letter.
b) The baby will be asleep	if he hasn't had a good night's sleep.
c) The car won't start	we'll go on a nice holiday.
d) If we've run out of milk	our parents will be very worried about him.
e) I won't watch the film on television	I'll go to the shops and buy some.
f) If you have done your homework by seven o'clock	I will apologise to her.
	we can catch a film at the cinema.
g) If Gordon has arrived by twelve o'clock	I'll make him some lunch.
h) If the post office has closed by the time we arrive	if it has already started.
i) If she hasn't finished cleaning her room she	if you haven't bothered to fill it with petrol.
j) If my brother hasn't arrived home by midnight	won't be able to hang out with her friends.
	I'll pour you another glass.
k) If the dog hasn't been fed yet	if you haven't finished cooking dinner yet.
l) If you've finished drinking your water	he'll jump up and down and whine and bark.
m) If we've saved enough money	if we've been quiet enough.
n) He will be in a terrible temper all day	
o) If I have been rude to Martha	

3.9 Zero Conditional vs First Conditional

What is the difference between Zero Conditional and First Conditional?

Zero Conditional is used to describe a general situation / general truth.
First Conditional is used to describe a specific situation in this moment.

Zero Conditional	First Conditional
If you study you get good marks. *(This is generally true.)*	If you study *(for the exams you have now)* you'll get good marks.
If you do physical exercise you get fit. *(This is generally true not just of you, a particular person, but for all people.)*	If you do physical exercise you'll get fit. *(I'm talking to you, specifically about your situation.)*
If I make a mess in the kitchen and don't clean it Mum gets angry at me. *(This is generally what happens when I don't clean up after myself.)*	If I make a mess in the kitchen and don't clean it Mum will get angry at me. *(I'm talking about a specific situation right now. I know what will happen if I don't clean up after myself now.)*

3.9.1 Write either a Zero Conditional or First Conditional sentence for each situation:

a) Your friend has only enough money to pay her rent but she wants to buy new clothes, too. It's not possible for her to do both.

   If you buy new clothes you won't have enough money to pay your rent.

b) People generally spend more money than they should and then they have problems later.

c) You're going to be late for work and your boss has been in a terrible temper lately.

d) Alice is always late for every job she has and she usually gets fired after a few months.

e) Polly wants to lose weight but she doesn't like exercise. Tell her what you think.

f) Most people want to lose weight but they don't like exercise.

g) Your friend is drinking his ninth vodka tonic and you think this is a bad plan.

h) Evelyn doesn't brush her teeth properly. Her teeth are a disaster and she's going to the dentist tomorrow.

i) A lot of people don't take care of their teeth and this causes big problems.

j) It's cold out and your sister wants to go outside without a sweater.

k) Maybe there's a good film playing at the cinema.

l) Sam is allergic to strawberries and he has just put fruit salad on his plate.

m) People who have diabetes should not eat sugary snacks.

n) Carla is very rude to all her friends and they are getting angry with her.

o) I might be hungry later on.

p) My house is very dirty and messy and I'm having friends over for dinner tonight.

3.10 First Conditional Sample Texts

a) I'll help you if you need help. If you need to ask questions or you just want to talk, I will be here for you. I won't tell anyone what you say unless it's ok with you. I won't judge you or make fun of you or laugh at your problems. I will listen to you when you speak. As soon as you talk about your problems you will see that sharing your burden makes you feel better.

b) I'm very angry with Oliver. I'm furious with him. Yesterday he took money out of my wallet without asking me. When I see him I'm going to shout at him. How could he do this to me? If he tries to deny it and say it wasn't him I will tell him that Ella saw him do it. Maybe he will be ashamed when he finds out that we all know he's a thief. Maybe he will be sorry that he hurt me. Probably he will deny it when I tell him I know what he did. Oliver is a person who never takes responsibility for his behaviour. If you ask him to be honest with you he'll do anything he can not to tell the truth. I'm finished with him. If he still wants to be my friend after today I'll tell him to leave me alone.

c) I'm going to go to Paris as soon as I can save enough money. If I work extra shifts I'll be able to save enough by Christmas. When I get to Paris I'm going to walk along the Seine and drink coffee in sidewalk cafes. I'm taking French lessons so I can speak to the people there. If my French is good enough maybe I'll make some new friends. As soon as I land in Paris I'm going to go shopping for some elegant clothes. I'll go to museums and eat in fancy restaurants. I had better work a lot if I'm going to do all these expensive things!

d) Don't tell lies or you'll get into trouble with people. Why do that to yourself? If you tell people stories all the time, after a while they won't believe you when you really are telling the truth. If you tell lies people will dislike and distrust you. If you tell the truth, you will never have to remember what you told to whom. If you tell lies you'll always have to think, "now what did I say to this person, or that person". If you tell the truth to people, you will be respected.

e) If you've finished your dinner by six thirty I'll pick you up and we'll go out for drinks afterwards. If you have to work early tomorrow morning we won't stay out late, I promise. I would like to go out and have some fun and maybe meet some people. If I see a nice looking man I might give him my phone number. Well, maybe not. Let's face it. Even if I give someone my phone number, they won't call me. No one ever calls someone they meet in a bar, do they? Anyway, if we go to that nice place over on Lincoln Street I'm going to order a martini. They make nice martinis. But if I drink a martini I won't be able to drive home afterwards. Maybe we should take a taxi to the club. If it's warm later on I'll wear my blue skirt and white top. If it's cold I'll wear my nice new jacket. I hope we have a good time!

4. Second Conditional

4.1   Forms

Second Conditional is used to talk about hypothetical situations or wishes. It is used to talk about things that probably won't happen, or things that we wish would happen at some point in the future. Why do we use the past form of the verb to express a hypothetical situation in the future? Who knows!!!

Because it is hypothetical, we never use **when / whenever / as soon as/ unless** like we can in Zero or First Conditional. We can only use "if".

Incorrect: *If ~~I would have~~ a million dollars I would buy a house.*

Correct: *If I had a million dollars I would buy a house.*

One "would" only"!!!

The form for Second Conditional is:

If + past verb + would (infinitive)

If condition	would consequence
If he lied to me	I would be very angry with him.
If my cat got sick	I would take him to the veterinarian.
If you did something stupid	I would tell you my opinion.

Examples

If I **had** a million dollars, I **would buy** a car. *(But I don't have a million dollars, so I am not able to buy a car.)*

If I **knew** the truth, I **would tell** you. *(But I don't know the truth, so I can't tell you anything.)*

If I **saw** a man from Mars, I **would run** away. *(But there are no men from Mars in my town, so I don't need to run away.)*

If I **found** money on the street, I **would buy** you a gift. *(Unfortunately, I haven't found money on the street so you don't get a gift from me.)*

If I **forgot** your birthday, I **would feel** very guilty. *(But I never forget your birthday, so I don't need to feel bad.)*

If you **hurt** me, I **wouldn't be** your friend anymore. *(But you haven't hurt me, so we are still friends.)*

4.1.1   Create some Second Conditional sentences using these ideas:

    a)   Win the lottery (for example... If I won the lottery I would take a very long holiday.)

    b)   Find a large amount of money

    c)   Date a famous person

    d)   Meet the Prime Minister

    e)   Build a time machine

    f)   Am a genius

    g)   Have a new car

    h)   Am very beautiful/handsome

    i)   Am a very good student

    j)   Am a politician

    k)   Travel at the speed of light

    l)   Become invisible

    m) Have enough time

    n)   Know the secrets of the universe

    o)   Meet an alien

    p)   Have a holiday house on the beach

4.1.2   You are having a conversation with Miss Down. Lucky you! She isn't very satisfied with her life. Fill in the correct form of Second Conditional.

You: Hello Miss Down, how are you?

Miss D: If I _____(am not feeling sick) I _____ (be better)

You: You're sick? I'm sorry to hear that. What would make you feel better?

Miss D: If I _____(have) some aspirin, my head _____(not hurt) so much.

You: Anything else?

Miss D: My nose is stuffed up and I can't breathe. If my nose _____(is stuffed up) I

_____(can breathe) better.

You: I understand.

Miss D: If I _____(can breathe) better I _____(be able to) sleep all night.

You: Of course.

Miss D: If I _____ (can sleep) I _____(not feel) so tired.

You: I see.

Miss D: And if I _____(am not so tired) I _____(feel) better.

You: Yes, of course.

Miss D: If I _____(have) a better jacket I _____ (be) warmer.

You: Oh. Ok.

Miss D: And if I _____(am) warmer I probably _____ (not have) a cold at all.

You: I think I have to go now.

Miss D: If I _____ (am) more interesting, people _____ (stay) and talk to me.

You: Ahem....

Miss D: Where are you going?

You: If I _____(have time) I _____(stay longer) but I have an appointment with my dentist! Bye!!!!

You can also express **Second Conditional** in this way:

would (infinitive)+ if + past verb

would consequence	If condition
I would be very angry with him.	if he lied to me
I would take my cat to the veterinarian.	if he got sick
I would tell you my opinion.	if you did something stupid

Remember! One would only!

Examples

I **would buy** a car **if** I **had** a million dollars.

I **would tell** you **if** I **knew** the truth.

I **would run** away **if** I **saw** a man from Mars.

I **would buy** you a gift **if** I **found** money on the street.

I **would feel** very guilty **if** I **forgot** your birthday.

I **wouldn't be** your friend anymore **if** you **hurt** me.

4.1.3   Create some Second Conditional sentences using the _if_ clause:

a) Jim would start to cry if you took away his beer.

b) My neighbour would be very angry

c) I would shop in all the most expensive places

d) We would travel the world

e) Frieda would have more friends

f) Olivia wouldn't be so unorganised

g) Mr. and Mrs. Jones would be happier

h) We wouldn't be angry

i) Ronald would go skiing every weekend

j) I would be more motivated

k) William would be in better physical condition

l) My team would win more games

m) The dog wouldn't bark and jump around so much

n) He would sleep better at night

o) I would run away screaming and shouting

p) You would be more successful

4.2   If I were

The First Person and Third person singular of the verb **to be** is **I was**. *(I was with my friends yesterday. She wasn't very happy. Was he here before?)*

When we use Second Conditional in First or Third Person singular we don't say **If I was/ If he was**. We say **If I were / If he/she/it were**.

This may be strange, but the sentence is in the subjunctive mood – this is used for hypothetical situations – and so it takes **were**. A sentence which expresses facts or asks a question is in the indicative mood and it takes **was**. Note the difference:

Indicative Mood (Facts / Questions)	Subjunctive Mood (Hypothetical situations)
If I was here before I don't remember. *(Is it a fact that I was here? I don't know, I don't remember)*	If I were you I wouldn't eat in this restaurant. *(I'm giving you advice based on my experience/ opinion.)*
If I saw her on Tuesday then I probably saw her at school. *(I'm not sure if I saw her, but if I did it was at school.)*	If I were in her place I would be very happy. *(She has a nice life. If I had her life I would be very pleased. Of course, I don't have her life. This is hypothetical.)*
If I was rude or impolite to you it was not my intention. *(Perhaps it is a fact that I was rude but I didn't intend to behave like this.)*	If I were as rude as she is I would be ashamed of myself. *(I am imagining what it would be like to be rude. I am not rude, so this is hypothetical.)*

The Second Conditional form for First Person and Third Person Singular is:

If I / he / she / it were + pronoun + would + infinitive

Hypothetical situation	Reality
If I were rich I would buy a new car	*But I have no money, so no new car.*
If he weren't so tired he would go jogging.	*But he is tired, so no jogging for him.*
If she were more motivated she would have a better job.	*But she isn't very motivated, so her job isn't very good.*

4.2.1   Finish these sentences using Second Conditional:

a) If I were rich

b) If I were younger

c) If I were old

d) If I were an alien from another planet

e) If I were more organised

f) If I were in better physical condition

g) If I were angry with someone

h) If I were feeling better

i) If I were a movie star

j) If I were about to buy a new car

k) If I were living in Paris

l) If I were in your situation

m) If I were any animal in the world

n) If I were a super hero

o) If I were a politician

4.3   If I were you / her / him etc.

To give someone advice in English we often tell them what we would do if we were in their position. Because this is hypothetical, we need to use the subjunctive mood – **if I were** and the object pronoun *(me, you, him, her, it, them, us, you)* The form is:

If I were + object pronoun + I would + infinitive

If can be used to give advice directly to someone using the object pronoun **you**:

If I were you I wouldn't smoke so much.

It can also be used to say what we would do if we were another person, not someone we are speaking to directly (gossip!):

If I were Angela I would be very happy. She has a great life.
If I were him I would be more careful with my work.

4.3.1   You are talking to your friends. Give advice or your opinion about what you would do if you were someone else:

a) My stomach really hurts. If I were you I would see a doctor.

b) Brandon makes very bad choices.

c) Gina tells a lot of lies to people.

d) I use the internet a lot at work and my boss is getting angry with me.

e) I eat a lot of cake.

f) Danny and Ray have been disrespectful to their parents.

g) His house is very dirty and messy.

h) She never eats any vegetables.

i) Shannon spends a lot of money but she doesn't have a very good job.

j) Theo eats pizza every night.

k) I never go to bed before three o'clock in the morning.

l) Hilary drinks a large cup of coffee at night and then she can't sleep.

m) Peter never takes any exercise.

n) My tooth hurts.

o) I'm bored.

p) Jane has a horrible boyfriend.

4.4 If you were me / her / him etc.

Sometimes we ask for advice as well as give it to others. In this case the form is:

If + Subject Pronoun + were + Object Pronoun + would + infinitive

If clause first	*would clause first*
If you were me, what would you do?	What would you do if you were me?
If you were her what would you do?	What would you do if you were her?
If you were me would you tell the truth?	Would you tell the truth if you were me?
If you were in my position what would you do?	What would you do if you were in my position?

4.4.1 Rewrite these sentences using Second Conditional for advice. Watch the pronouns!

a) Rachel is asking you what you would do if you were in her position. *What would you do if you were me?*

b) Frances is asking you what Theo should do.

c) Gerry is asking you what his father should do.

d) Ronald and Andrew are asking you what they should do.

e) I am asking you what I should do.

f) Hilary is asking you what Polly should do.

g) Ella is asking you what Oliver should do.

h) Finn is asking you what David should do.

i) William is asking you what James should do.

j) Kate is asking what you would do.

k) Kate is asking you what Emma should do.

l) Ask your mum for her opinion about your situation.

m) Ask your mum for her opinion about your sister's situation.

n) Ask your mum for her opinion about your friends' situation. (*plural!*)

o) Ask your boss for his opinion about your colleagues. *(plural!)*

p) Ask your husband for his opinion about the Prime Minister's situation.

4.5   What would you do if...

Second Conditional is often used to answer the hypothetical question "**what would you do if?**"

What would you do if + past verb + object?	What would you do if you had a lot of money?
(If clause) + I would infinitive + answer	If I had a lot of money I would buy a new car.
	I would buy a new car.

You can also cut the 'if clause' out of your answer:

What would you do if + past verb + object?	What would you do if you saw a bank robbery?
I would infinitive + answer	I would call the police.

4.5.1   Answer these questions using Second Conditional

a)   What would you do if you were a great singer? *I would give concerts all over the world.*

b)   What would you do if you found a bag full of money on the street?

c)   What would you say if you met your favourite actor?

d)   Where would you go if you could go anywhere in the world?

e)   What would you eat for your last ever dinner?

f)   If you had a different job, what would it be?

g)   If you changed your life right now, what would you do?

h)   If you saw a UFO, what would you do?

i)   If you had a lot of money, what kind of car would you drive?

j)   If you had a lot of time, what would you do?

k)   If you were the boss, what would you change?

l)   If you had a super-power, what would it be?

m) If you saw your best friend's husband with another woman, would you tell?

n) If you knew a big secret about a person you didn't like, would you keep the secret or tell everyone?

o) What would you do if you had unlimited time and unlimited money?

p) If you had a time machine, what would you do?

4.6   Could

You can also make Second Conditional sentences using **could** instead of **would**. There is a slight difference in meaning. **Would** indicates something you have the intention of doing. **Could** indicates something that is a possibility, but there may be other possibilities as well. The form is:

If + past simple verb + could + infinitive

Would	Could
If he came over to my house I would cook him dinner. (Cooking dinner is the thing that I would do.)	If he came over to my house I could cook him dinner. (It's a possibility. I could also order a pizza or make sandwiches.
If you helped me I would buy you a gift. (If you help me you will receive a gift.)	If you helped me I could buy you a gift. (I might possibly buy you a gift but it's not 100% sure that I will.
If we had enough money we would buy a car. (The only thing stopping us from buying a car is that we don't have enough money.)	If we had enough money we could buy a car. (It would be a possibility, but we might also choose to take a nice holiday.)

4.6.1   Match the sentences:

a) If I had more money	if we really wanted to.
b) If you were nicer to people	I could buy whatever I wanted.
c) If I were in better physical shape	you could have more friends.
d) I could concentrate on this problem better	the baby could sleep.
e) If my house were more organised	if we found a cheap flight.
f) If she dressed more professionally	if he studied harder.
g) If they didn't spend money like drunken sailors	I could run a marathon.
	if he weren't so socially awkward.
h) If you worked less you	I could find my keys and bag more easily.
i) If we woke up earlier in the morning	if you stopped talking so loudly.
j) If you didn't turn the television up so loud	

k) If the weather were nicer	they could have more in the bank.
l) We could go to London	could spend more time with your family.
m) Evan could do better in school	we could get more done during the day.
n) We could change our lives	we could go for a walk today.
o) George could have a girlfriend	she could find a better job.

4.7   Might

Might can also be used in Second Conditional. Where **would** is more definite in nature and **could** indicates that there is more than one possibility, **might** can be used to mean maybe something will happen and maybe it won't. **Could** gives the idea that more than one thing could happen. **Might** does not indicate other possibilities, it indicates the possibility of something happening or not happening. The form is:

If + past verb + might (not) + infinitive

If we had more time we might not feel so stressed.
If you woke up earlier you might get to work on time.

Would	Could	Might
If he came over to my house I would cook him dinner. (Cooking dinner is the thing that I would do.)	If he came over to my house I could cook him dinner. (It's a possibility. I could also order a pizza or make sandwiches.	If he came over to my house I might cook him dinner. (Then again, I might not.)
If you helped me I would buy you a gift. (If you help me you will receive a gift.)	If you helped me I could buy you a gift. (I might possibly buy you a gift or maybe take you out for dinner.)	If you helped me I might buy you a gift. (Or I might not buy you a gift.)
If we had enough money we would buy a car. (The only thing stopping us from buying a car is that we don't have enough money.)	If we had enough money we could buy a car. (It would be a possibility, but we might also choose to take a nice holiday.)	If we had enough money we might buy a car. (Or we might do nothing with the money.)

4.7.1   Finish the sentences using Second Conditional with might.

a) If the TV repairman came over to fix our television, *we might be able to watch the football match.*

b) You want to go out this evening. If you did all your homework before six o'clock

c) Diane has problems with her job. If she put more effort into her work

d) Your stomach hurts. If you didn't eat so quickly

e) You're sad and depressed. If went out with your friends more often

f) Your hair looks horrible. If you got a hair-cut

g) You have a headache. If you took an aspirin

h) I'm afraid to tell my friend how I feel. If I told her how I felt

i) Kevin drinks too much. If he didn't drink so much

j) Our garden looks horrible. If we took more care with the garden

k) If you didn't spend all your money the first day you got paid

l) If Larry was kinder and more polite to people

m) Sam smokes heavily and he has a difficult time walking. If he didn't smoke so much

n) Arnold spends too much time on his computer. If he spent less time on the internet

o) Dan isn't very successful. If he worked harder

p) Michael meets horrible women in nightclubs. If he met normal women

4.8   Could and Would Together

Could and **would** can also go together in a Second Conditional Sentence. **Could** goes with the **if** clause and **would** goes with the result. This form of Second Conditional is often used to talk about what we wish we could do if the conditions were right. The form is:

If + could (not) + infinitive + would (not) + infinitive

If clause	Result Clause
If I could sing	I would sing in night clubs. (But I can't sing, I'm terrible, so I will stay away from the night clubs.)
If I couldn't run in races	I would be very sad. (But I can run so I'm not sad.)
Even if I could help you	I wouldn't. (I don't like you. I'm not able to help you but if I were, too bad for you, I wouldn't.)

4.8.1   What would you do if you could?

a)   If I could have one super power *I would fly.*

b)   If I could go anywhere in the world

c)   If I could meet anyone from history

d)   If we could buy anything we wanted

e)   If I could take a holiday

f)   If I could find my keys

g)   If she could walk faster

h)   If I could find more time

i)   If I could draw really well

j)   If I could play any sport

k)   If I could cook very well

l)   If I could have any job in the world

m) If I could hack into any website

n) If we could take the whole summer off and not work

o) If we could stop arguing and fighting

p) If I could have a conversation with my dog

4.9   Second Conditional with Continuous Subjunctive

Second Conditional can also be expressed using Present Continuous Subjunctive. This is usually used to talk about an unreal situation which would be happening (but is not) at the time of speaking. You will often find the words **now, right now, at the moment** in these sentences. The form is:

Would be + verb(ing) + if + Past Simple

I **would be sitting** on a beach right **now if** I **weren't** at work.	But I am at work right now. Bad luck for me.
Mary **would be coming** to the beach with us **today if** it **weren't** for her job.	Mary has to work so she can't come with us.
I **wouldn't be living** in this flat **if** it **weren't** for your help.	You helped me find this flat and now I am living here.

4.9.1   Finish these sentences using the verb in bold and Present Continuous Subjunctive:

a) It's three o'clock in the morning and I can't **sleep**. If it weren't for my noisy neighbours *I would be sleeping right now.*

b) All my friends are **skiing** in the mountains but my parents won't let me go. If it weren't for my parents

c) We arrived at the cinema too late to **watch** the film. If it weren't for being late

d) I have no food in my fridge because I forgot to go to the shops. Now I have nothing to **cook**. If it weren't for me

e) Donald has to work instead of **going** out with his friends. If it weren't for his boss

f) Gina would love to **work** as an architect but she can't find a job. If it weren't for the job market

g) Ray has to take the bus to work instead of **driving** his car because he had a minor car accident. If it weren't for the accident

h) We wanted to **stay** in this hotel but they were full. If they weren't full

i) Sam doesn't **feel** well because he has a cold. If it weren't for his cold

j) I broke my leg so I can't **train** for the marathon. If it weren't for my broken leg

k) Our dog ate the steaks we bought for lunch and now we are **eating** sandwiches. If it weren't for that crazy dog

l) Henry had the chance to **date** a supermodel but he's an idiot. If he weren't such an idiot

m) I dropped my phone in the lake and now it won't **work**. If I weren't such a clumsy person

n) Martin wanted to go for a bike **ride** but his tire is flat. If it weren't flat

o) She wants to **relax** in front of the TV but she can't because she has an exam. If it weren't for that exam

p) I ate too many sweets and now my tooth **hurts**. If I weren't so greedy

4.10 Implied "If" Clause

Sometimes we use Second Conditional without using the **if** clause. In these cases, the **if** clause is understood by the person to whom we are speaking. The form is:

Pronoun + Would + Infinitive

Did you see how rude Michelle was to Jane? I **would be** so angry.	I would be angry if I were in Jane's position.
You are very late. **I would leave** right now.	You are late. I would leave now if I were you.
Did you hear that Edith is moving to New York? I **would be** so happy!	I would be so happy if I were Edith.

4.10.1 Match the situations with the implied if clause.

a) Did you see how much Kelly eats? Incredible!	I would burn everything.
b) You ran 25 km today?	I would cry.
c) Hilary didn't get the promotion her boss promised her after all the work she did.	I would take it back the shop.
	I would be so angry!
d) Allen's daughter won the music competition.	I would go over to her house and ask her what the problem is.
e) Nigel drank fifteen glasses of beer last night.	
f) You haven't slept properly in a week?	I would be so proud!
g) His brother is the best at everything and Larry is a bit of a loser.	I would be so tired!
h) I can't understand Bob. He can never find anything and he's always late.	I would have a huge headache.
	I would go to the dentist.
i) Sandra charges three dollars an hour to clean houses.	I would complain to the boss.
j) Charlie is a brilliant chef. His cakes are fantastic.	I would ask for more money.
k) Virginia has been complaining for weeks that her tooth hurts	I would be exhausted!

her.	I would be very fat!
l) Your co-worker took your idea and said it was his?	I would be so envious.
m) David bought an expensive new television and after one week it was broken.	I would be more organised.
n) Annie won't return your phone calls?	
o) No one came to Nancy's birthday party.	

4.11 Implied "If" Clause for Questions

Second Conditional without the **if** clause can be used to ask hypothetical, rhetorical questions for which there is no answer, or the answer is impossible or obvious. The form is

Who/ What/When/Where/Why/How + Would + Pronoun + Infinitive

You are wonderful! **What would we do** without you?	Lucky for us, this is hypothetical. We don't have to worry because you are here.
I have six dogs. I can't move to a new apartment. **Where would I go**?	It would be impossible to find a flat that would let me keep six dogs.
Why would you do such a stupid thing?	That was stupid or horrible. What were you thinking?

4.11.1 Ask some Second Conditional questions in response to these conversation topics using the verb in parenthesis.

a) Your friend is talking about how she wishes she could take a trip around the world. (go) Where
    would you go?

b) Kelly thinks she might win two tickets for a concert. (take) Who

c) Tanya would love to have a pet. (get) What kind

d) Phillip dreams about moving to a new country. (live) Where

e) Don wishes he had a million dollars. (spend) How

f) Frieda would like to change jobs. (do) What

g) Simon wishes he could play a musical instrument. (play) which

h) George would love to meet an alien from another planet. (say) What

i) Ryan wants a big family. (have) How many

j) Amber is angry at her friend and wishes she could tell her how angry she is. (say) What

k) Your husband is dreaming of building a big, expensive house. (pay) How

l) Kevin wishes he had a time machine. (meet) Who

m) Louisa would love to go back to university. (study) What

n) Jill dreams of having her own shop. (sell) What

o) Theo worries his boss will find out he's been stealing money from the company. (explain) How

p) James is sixteen and he wants to move out and live on his own. (manage) How

4.12 Making a wish

When we make a wish in English we use **Second Conditional** to express something we wish would happen in the present / future. The form is:

Pronoun + Wish + Pronoun + Past Simple Verb

Situation	Present / Future Wish
I don't have any time.	I wish I had more time.
I don't know her.	I wish I knew her.
I'm not very fit.	I wish I were fit. *
He talks very loudly	I wish he didn't talk so loudly.

*Don't forget we use the Subjunctive - "I were" instead of "I was"

4.12.1 Here are some situations. Write them as wishes in the present/ future and the past.

    a) My job is terrible.

    b) The weather is horrible.

    c) We are very busy.

    d) He would like a girlfriend.

    e) This is very complicated.

    f) I eat too much.

    g) It's too hot outside.

    h) My neighbour is completely crazy.

    i) This project is very difficult.

    j) She is very angry.

    k) They hate their apartment.

    l) I have the flu.

    m) I'm allergic to dogs.

    n) The dinner I cooked is disgusting.

    o) I'm horrible at Maths.

4.13 First Conditional vs Second Conditional

First Conditional is used to talk about situations which are normal, probably and very likely to happen. Second Conditional is used to talk about hypothetical situations and situations which will probably never happen.

Here is how First Conditional is different from Second Conditional in everyday conversation:

Imagine that Tom is a Hollywood executive. He works with all the big, important movie stars. He knows everyone and he goes to all the parties. He's talking with his friend about a famous movie star.

*If **I see** him, **I'll invite** him to my party.*

This is quite normal for Tom, he probably knows a lot of famous movie stars very well. It's not unusual for him to meet people like this.

Now, imagine that you live in a small town. You work in a shop that sells ice cream. You say to your best friend:

*If I **see** a famous movie star, **I'll** invite him to my party.*

Probably your friend will think that you are crazy if you say this. You don't know anyone from Hollywood and unless they came to your small town and into your shop to buy ice cream, you don't have a chance to meet any.

If you told your friend:

*If I **saw** a movie star, **I'd invite** him to my party.*

Your friend will understand that you are talking about something hypothetical, not very probable and is less likely to think you are crazy. ☺

First Conditional (Hollywood Executive)	*Second Conditional* (Small town ice-cream shop worker)
If we're going to the party we will take a limousine.	If I were going to a party I would take a limousine.
If this house doesn't have a swimming pool I won't buy it.	If I were rich I would have a house with a swimming pool.
If we have time we could go skiing in the Alps for the weekend.	If I could, I would go skiing in the Alps for the weekend.

4.14 Second Conditional Sample Texts

a) If I were you I would be more organised. Look at your house! It's a disaster zone! I would wash the dishes and put away my clothes, if I were you. What would you do if you had company come to your house and they saw this mess? Wouldn't you be embarrassed if someone saw this? I would be very unhappy if I lived like this. You have old food on the counters and rubbish everywhere. If your landlord saw this he would be very unhappy with you. If he came here and saw this mess you might have to find a new place to live.

b) Jenny called me yesterday and asked me to go out with her tonight. I don't want to go. If I went out with her it would be a disaster. Jenny is always doing something stupid crazy things are always happening to her. If we went out we would be kidnapped by aliens from another planet. We would take a wrong turning and end up in Belgium. We would get into a fight in a bar and get arrested. My point is that Jenny is crazy and going out with her always ends badly. If I told you the kinds of things she does, you wouldn't believe me.

c) What would you do if you found a big bag of money on the train? If it were me, I would probably call the police and tell them I found the money. Someone would be very unhappy if they lost a big bag of money and I wouldn't want someone else to be unhappy. But if I did take the money to the police that would be stupid because they would probably take the money and go to Mexico. Maybe I wouldn't call the police after all. Maybe I would go shopping and buy some new clothes and some jewellery. But if I took the money and didn't call the police I would probably feel guilty and horrible. If I felt guilty and horrible I wouldn't even enjoy spending the money. If I had all that money and I didn't enjoy spending it, then I guess I would have to take it to the police. Sometimes, being honest sucks.

d) Lisa would like to go to university in Paris but there's a problem. She doesn't speak French very well. If she spoke French she would be going to school in Paris right now, but she doesn't. She takes lessons but she doesn't do her homework. If she did her homework she would improve her French. If she improved her French she would be closer to her goal of going to university in Paris. The truth is that Lisa's a very busy person. She works two jobs and has a lot of hobbies. If she had fewer obligations she might be able to dedicate more time to studying.

e) If I could do anything in the world, I would end world hunger and war. I would insist that big corporations pay their taxes and politicians tell the truth. If I could, I would make the world a safer place to be. I would make sure that everyone had the chance to go to school and eat good food and live in a safe, secure home. I would catch dangerous criminals and put them on a rocket and send them to the moon.

f) What would you do if you saw your best friend's husband with another woman? I think if it were me, I would tell her what I saw. If you didn't tell her that I saw her husband with another woman and she found out later that I knew, she would be very hurt. Then again, if I told her and she didn't want to know she might get very angry with me. Sometimes people react badly when they hear bad news. If she got upset she might yell at me, even though it isn't my fault. I think what I'm going to do instead is break my glasses so I never see anyone, anywhere. It's safer that way.

5. Third Conditional

5.1   Forms

Zero, First and Second Conditional are concerned with the possible present and future (likely or unlikely). Third Conditional is the only conditional that describes situations which happened (or didn't happen) in the past.

The form for Third Conditional is:

If + (past perfect) + would/could have (past participle)

Past Event	Consequence
If I hadn't eaten so much	I wouldn't have been sick.
If you had been honest	your friends would have understood.
If we had known the hotel was so expensive	we wouldn't have told you to stay there.

If I had known *you were coming,* ***I would have cleaned*** *my house.* (But I didn't know you were coming, so I didn't clean my house)

If we had arrived *on time,* ***we wouldn't have missed*** *the first part of the film.* (But we arrived late, so we missed the first part of the film)

If she had studied *for that exam,* ***she would have passed****.* (But she didn't study, so she failed.)

If he had earned *enough money,* ***he would have bough****t a house.* (He wanted to buy a house but he didn't have the money.)

Students often have trouble with Third Conditional. It's not complicated but you do have to remember all the parts of the sentence. It may help to think of Third Conditional sentences as having seven parts:

If	Pronoun	Past Perfect	Condition	Pronoun	Would Have +Past Participle	Result
If	you	had finished	on time	we	wouldn't have been	late.

5.1.1 Read the sentences and then express the situation in Third Conditional.

a) My brother told my mum I was smoking cigarettes so I hit him.

If	Pronoun	Past Perfect	Condition	Pronoun	Would Have +Past Participle	Result
If	he	hadn't told	my mum	I	wouldn't have hit	him

b) I drank too much coffee and I felt sick.

If	Pronoun	Past Perfect	Condition	Pronoun	Would Have +Past Participle	Result

c) I dropped my phone and it was broken.

If	Pronoun	Past Perfect	Condition	Pronoun	Would Have +Past Participle	Result

d) I left my book outside. It rained and the book was ruined.

If	Pronoun	Past Perfect	Condition	Pronoun	Would Have +Past Participle	Result

e) I didn't brush my teeth carefully and I got cavities.

If	Pronoun	Past Perfect	Condition	Pronoun	Would Have +Past Participle	Result

f) I spilled coffee on my new shirt and it stained.

If	Pronoun	Past Perfect	Condition	Pronoun	Would Have +Past Participle	Result

g) George forgot to call me and I got angry with him.

If	Pronoun	Past Perfect	Condition	Pronoun	Would Have +Past Participle	Result

h) Barbara missed the bus and was late for work.

If	Pronoun	Past Perfect	Condition	Pronoun	Would Have +Past Participle	Result

i) The bank was closed so I didn't take out any money.

If	Pronoun	Past Perfect	Condition	Pronoun	Would Have +Past Participle	Result

j) I didn't finish my work so I didn't go out with my friends.

If	Pronoun	Past Perfect	Condition	Pronoun	Would Have +Past Participle	Result

k) I left the milk on the kitchen table and it went bad.

If	Pronoun	Past Perfect	Condition	Pronoun	Would Have +Past Participle	Result

l) I told my friend my real opinion about her new boyfriend and she got angry with me.

If	Pronoun	Past Perfect	Condition	Pronoun	Would Have +Past Participle	Result

m) Bill forgot to pay his electric bill. The electricity was turned off.

If	Pronoun	Past Perfect	Condition	Pronoun	Would Have +Past Participle	Result

n) Sally left her handbag on the bus and someone stole her money and identification.

If	Pronoun	Past Perfect	Condition	Pronoun	Would Have +Past Participle	Result

o) I met Alex and he inspired me to become a doctor.

If	Pronoun	Past Perfect	Condition	Pronoun	Would Have +Past Participle	Result

p) I was late coming home last night and I missed your call.

If	Pronoun	Past Perfect	Condition	Pronoun	Would Have +Past Participle	Result

q) I wasn't paying attention while I was driving and I got into a car accident.

If	Pronoun	Past Perfect	Condition	Pronoun	Would Have +Past Participle	Result

r) Greg told a lie and got into trouble.

If	Pronoun	Past Perfect	Condition	Pronoun	Would Have +Past Participle	Result

s) Zoe forgot to feed her fish and it died.

If	Pronoun	Past Perfect	Condition	Pronoun	Would Have +Past Participle	Result

5.1.2 Take the following situations and express them in Third Conditional:

a) You bought a car and there are a lot of problems with the car. You didn't know about the problems when you bought the car and now you are sorry.

b) You didn't go shopping for food this afternoon, and some of your friends came to your house without calling first. You had guests and nothing to feed them.

c) You bought expensive clothes and now you don't have the money to pay your rent. You were sorry.

d) You ate something that made you sick.

e) You told your friend a secret and he told everyone.

f) You forgot your mother's birthday and she was upset with you.

g) Your friend broke the law and then she had legal problems.

h) Your brother was divorced last year. He was sorry he married the wrong woman.

i) You went to university and learned some very interesting things. You are thinking about what life would have been like if you hadn't been to university.

j) You were talking on the phone and you didn't notice that your dinner was burning on the stove.

k) You got a terrible haircut before your school photos.

l) You studied very hard for an exam, and you were grateful because the exam was very difficult, but you passed.

m) Most of your friends didn't study for that exam, and they didn't pass.

n) You watched a film on television until three o'clock in the morning and you were late for work the next morning.

o) Your friend came over for dinner and you made chicken. You didn't know he was a vegetarian.

5.1.3 You are having a conversation with Mr. Unlucky. Fill in the gaps with Third Conditional.

You: Oh hello! What's new?

Mr. U: Oh, I'm in a terrible mess.

You: Really?

Mr. U: I was in a car accident and I destroyed my car.

You: Oh dear. That's awful.

Mr. U: I know… it's my fault. I was sending a text message while I was driving. If _____ (**not send**) a message I (not get) into an accident.

You: I suppose so.

Mr. U: I hit a fire hydrant and it exploded, and there was water all over the street. If I _____ (**not hit**) the fire hydrant, the street _____ (**not be**) flooded with water.

You: Oh, wow.

Mr. U: And then the police came. I was nervous so I was rude to the police man.

You: Oh, that's not a good idea.

Mr. U: I know. If I (**not shouted**) at the policeman, I _____ (**not be**) arrested.

You: You were arrested?

Mr. U: Yes, and that's not all. I was taken to the judge and told I had to pay a fine. But I didn't have any money. If _____ (**have the money**) I _____ (**not have to**) spend the night in jail.

You: Oh dear.

Mr. U: And if I _____ (**not spend**) the night in jail, I _____ (**not be**) late for work the next morning.

You: Oh my.

Mr. U: And if I _____ (**not be late**) for work I _____ (**not be**) fired from my job.

You: Wow.

Mr. U: And if I _____ (**not be**) fired from my job, I _____ (**be able**) to pay my rent.

You: Oh no.

Mr. U: Yes. And if I (**be able**) to pay my rent, I _____ (**not be**) thrown out of my apartment.

You: Oh dear.

Mr. U: Do you think I could stay at your house? I can sleep on the sofa!

You: Um, I think I can hear my mother calling me! Have to go! Bye!

Just as in the other Conditional forms, it is possible to express **Third Conditional** in reverse. The form is:

Would have + past participle + if + past perfect

Examples

I would have cleaned my house if I had known you were coming.

We wouldn't have missed the first part of the film if we had arrived on time.

She would have passed if she had studied for that exam.

He would have bought a house if he had earned enough money.

5.1.4   Finish these sentences using Past Perfect

a)   I would have helped you if

b)   I wouldn't have said such a stupid thing if

c)   He would have tried harder if

d)   We would have slept better if

e)   Sandra wouldn't have missed the bus if

f)   Peter would have won the competition if

g)   Ella would have been able to speak German better if

h)   They wouldn't have been so angry with you if

i)   I wouldn't have had a headache if

j)   Luke wouldn't have had legal problems if

k)   I wouldn't have locked my keys inside my car if

l)   We wouldn't have been late for the film if

m)   George would have had better luck with girls if

n)   Henry would have known the truth if

o)   Jane would have had more friends at school if

5.2   Had had

The Past Perfect tense is formed with **Had** and the Past Participle of the verb. It might seem strange, but to make the Past Perfect with the verb **to have** we use **had had.** The form is:

Pronoun + Had + Had + Object

Pronoun + Hadn't + Had + Object

Though it might seem strange, **hadn't had** is correct. Because it is awkward to say **had had**, in spoken English we usually use the contraction **'d**. It's simply pronounced by adding a soft **ed** sound to the end of the word. (This soft **ed** sounds like *mud*.)

Do not stress the *ed* sound! If the word ends in a vowel, the sound is not so much **ed**, but a simple **d.**

Julia'd had a big breakfast that morning. *(Juliad)*	Julia had had a big breakfast that morning.
Mark'd had a very bad day. *(Mark-ed)*	Mark had had a very bad day.
We'd had no luck finding our way without a map. *(Weed)*	We had had no luck finding our way without a map.

5.2.1   Practice these sentences out loud to get comfortable using 'd had. This exercise is about pronunciation **– we don't actually write this way.**

a) She'd [*Sheed*] had a fantastic time on holiday.

b) You'd [*Youd*] had your coffee first thing in the morning.

c) Jenn'd [*Jenn-ed*] had problems with her car.

d) They'd [*Theyd*] had dinner in a lovely restaurant.

e) I'd [*Eyed*] had something to eat that was making me sick.

f) Henry'd [*Henreed*] had a few different jobs before he found this one.

g) Martin'd [*Martin-ed*] had a flat tire on his bicycle.

h) My friends'd [*friends-ed*] had a party.

i) Greg'd [*Greg-ed*] had some very good luck.

j) Mrs. Smith'd [*Smith-ed*] had several strange telephone calls.

5.3   Third Conditional with Could

Could can be used in place of **would** in Third Conditional sentences. There is a difference in meaning between **could** and **would**. **Would** indicates something you have the intention of doing. **Could** indicates something that is a possibility or ability, but it is not guaranteed that would happen. The form is:

If + Past Perfect verb + could + have + Past Participle

Would	Could
If I had known he was alone I would have invited him over to my house.	If I had known he was alone I could have invited him to my house. (Or I could have gone to his house, met him in a restaurant, gone to the cinema....)
If she had organised her holiday better she would have had a better time.	If she had organised her holiday better she could have had a better time. (There is no guarantee that she would have had fun, but it could have happened.)
If we had been hungry we would have stopped and bought something to eat.	If we had been hungry we could have stopped and bought something to eat. (Or we could have gone home and made a sandwich, or had nothing at all.)

5.3.1 Match the sentences

a) If we'd had more time in London	they could have had a better marriage.
b) If I had worked harder when I was in school	he could have made a cake.
c) You could have arrived home a lot faster	we all could have received a fantastic pay rise.
d) If they had been more honest with each other	they could have caught the criminal.
	I could have avoided an expensive trip to the dentist.
e) If I'd taken better care of my teeth	
f) If you hadn't been busy on Saturday	you could have come to my birthday party.
g) Jerry could have been chosen for the basketball team	if he hadn't hurt his leg.
	if my husband hadn't been allergic to animals.
h) If I hadn't been obligated to go to my aunt's house for dinner	we could have visited the museums.
i) If the police had been given the information	I could have given you a lift home.
	if we hadn't been so tired.
j) Laura could have come to visit us for a week	if you had taken the bus instead of walked.
k) If I had known your car was being repaired	I could have become a doctor.
l) If our company had signed that contract	if she hadn't been so busy with work.
m) We could have gone out on Friday night	I could have come to your party.
n) If he'd had flour and eggs	
o) We could have got a dog	

5.4 Third Conditional with Might

Third Conditional can also be expressed using **might** instead of **would** or **could.** In this case, **might** will be used to say that maybe something happened. The form is:

If + Past Perfect + might have + Past Participle

If + Past Perfect + might not have + Past Participle

Would	Could	Might
If we'd had more time we would have visited the museum. (It was our intention but we weren't able to.)	If we'd had more time we could have visited the museum. (It would have been possible.)	If we'd had more time we might have visited the museum. (Maybe we would have visited the museum or maybe not.)
If she hadn't been driving so fast she would have avoided the accident. (I know for a fact that the accident wouldn't have happened.)	If she hadn't been driving so fast she could have avoided the accident. (It is possible that the whole thing could have been avoided.)	If she hadn't been driving so fast she might have avoided the accident. (Maybe the accident wouldn't have happened.)
If I had taken my medication I wouldn't have had a headache. (I know that my headache wouldn't have happened.)	If I had taken my medication I couldn't have had a headache. (It would have been impossible for me to get a headache.)	If I had taken my medication I might not have had a headache. * (Maybe the headache wouldn't have happened.)

5.4.1 Finish these sentences using might have done / might not have done

a) I wasn't paying attention and I lost my wallet on the bus. If I had been paying attention I might not have lost my wallet on the bus.

b) I forgot to go to the mechanic for a regular inspection and now my car needs serious repairs.

c) Eddie never ate fruit and vegetables and now he's sick.

d) Julia took too many pain tablets over the years and now they don't work for her anymore.

e) I left my bedroom window open and thieves broke into my house and stole my television.

f) Harold usually went to the same restaurant for lunch every day. One day he went to a different place and he met the woman he later married.

g) I read an interesting book about ancient Greece and it inspired me to become an archaeologist.

h) Lila broke her foot. She didn't listen to the doctor's advice about resting and the foot took much longer to get better.

i) My cousin decided to try a yoga class and he loved it. Now he's a yoga instructor.

j) The police found an important clue, solved the case and caught the criminal.

k) Bob helped a man on the street who had fallen and hurt himself. It was such an incredible experience that he started working in emergency medicine.

l) I went for a walk one night and happened to see a beautiful house for sale. I bought it.

m) I was talking to my aunt one day and she told me a story about my grandmother I had never heard before.

n) I was hungry one night and went into the first restaurant I saw. I loved the food and it became my new favourite place to go.

o) We learned the truth about the situation and decided to defend our friend.

p) Mary watched a cooking show on TV and found it interesting. She became a chef.

5.5   Past Perfect Continuous

Third Conditional can be expressed using Past Perfect Continuous instead of Past Perfect. This is used when the past action was continuous. The continuous action can be something that was happening over a long time or something that happened over a short time. The form is:

Past Perfect Continuous + Would / Could Have + Past Participle

Past Perfect Continuous + Wouldn't / Couldn't Have + Past Participle

If you hadn't been talking so loudly she wouldn't have heard the nasty things you said.	You were talking, loud and for too long and she heard you and now there's a problem.
If he had been doing his job properly we wouldn't have this crisis now.	He was not doing his job properly for a while and the result was a crisis.
If I hadn't been training for a long time I couldn't have run the marathon.	I was training for a long time and this helped me run the marathon.

5.5.1   Write sentences using Third Conditional with Past Perfect Continuous. Use the underlined verbs.

a) I was <u>sleeping</u> and I missed the television show. If I hadn't been sleeping I wouldn't have missed the TV show.

b) I was <u>studying</u> and I couldn't go to the party.

c) It was <u>snowing</u> for days and the skiing was fantastic.

d) We were <u>arguing</u> loudly and we didn't understand each other.

e) Alice was <u>listening</u> to music and couldn't hear her phone ring.

f) Molly was <u>recovering</u> from the flu and couldn't go camping.

g) Oliver was really <u>trying</u> hard so his teacher gave him some extra points.

h) Jen was <u>talking</u> constantly and no one else could participate in the conversation.

i) It was <u>raining</u> hard and the garden was flooded with water.

j) Marlene was <u>learning</u> Mandarin and she made friends with some nice people from Beijing.

k) I was <u>working</u> and couldn't go home early.

l) She was <u>feeling</u> anxious and couldn't sleep at night.

m) Kevin was <u>drinking</u> and he got into a car accident.

n) I was <u>staying</u> with my friends for the summer and they taught me how to cook.

o) Dad was <u>cooking</u> dinner and he couldn't help me with my homework.

p) Ella was <u>looking</u> at an old picture of her family when she saw something strange.

5.6 Third Conditional as Regret

Third Conditional can be used to express regret over something that did (or didn't) happen in the past. The form is:

*If + Past Perfect + + Would / Wouldn't Have Past Participle

If + Past Perfect + + Could / Couldn't Have + Past Participle

You can also express regret using Third Conditional by saying **If only and **I wish** which are discussed in the following chapters.*

If I had known you were having a difficult time I could have helped you.	I regret not knowing you were having a difficult time because it would have been possible for me to help you.
If I had done better on my exam I could have gone to medical school.	I regret not doing better on my exams because I missed the opportunity to go to medical school.
If I hadn't been so slow I could have arrived at the post office before they closed.	I regret being slow because I arrived too late at the post office.

5.6.1 Express regret using Third Conditional

a) You lost your keys and had to pay a lot of money to get someone to open your door. If I hadn't lost my keys I wouldn't have had to pay a lot of money to get someone to open the door.

b) You didn't know your brother was having medical problems so you didn't help him.

c) There was a great film playing at the cinema and you missed it because you had to go to a birthday party.

d) You bought a pair of expensive shoes and after you had no money.

e) You didn't know what size shirt your friend wears and you bought her the wrong one.

f) You ate something bad and it made you sick.

g) Your friend asked you not to tell a secret and you told everyone and she got angry at you.

h) You weren't able to go to the theatre with your friends because you were working.

i) You didn't know the electricity had gone out and all the food in your fridge spoiled.

j)   Your bicycle tire got a puncture and you couldn't go for a bike ride on Saturday.

k)   You didn't know your friend was allergic to fish and you made salmon for dinner.

l)   You accidentally threw out some old papers and later discovered they were very important.

m) You drank too much, got drunk and told your boss what you really thought of him.

n)   Your phone fell on the floor and broke and you had to buy a new one.

o)   The coffee was too hot. You drank it and burned your mouth.

p)   You stayed up late and watched a stupid film on TV and were very tired the next day.

5.7 Making a wish

When we make a wish in English we use **Second Conditional** for something we wish *would happen* in the present / future and **Third Conditional** for something we wish *had happened* in the past. Third Conditional can be used to express regret or disappointment about something that did or didn't happen in the past.

Second Conditional	Third Conditional
If + past verb + would do	If + past perfect + would have done
If I *saw* him I *would say* hello.	If I *had seen* him I *would have said* hello.

Situation	Present / Future Wish	Past Wish
I don't have any time.	I wish I had more time.	I wish I had had more time. (I wish I'd had more time.)
I don't know her.	I wish I knew her.	I wish I had known her. (I wish I'd known her.)
I'm not very fit.	I wish I were fit. *	I wish I had been fit. (I wish I'd been fit.)
He talks very loudly.	I wish he didn't talk so loudly.	I wish he hadn't talked so loudly.

* Instead of saying "I was" we say "I were" to express the Subjunctive

5.7.1 Write about these situations using I wish + Third Conditional. (Compare these answers to those in Chapter 4.12 – Making a Wish with Second Conditional)

a) My job was terrible.

b) The weather was horrible.

c) We were very busy.

d) This was very complicated.

e) I ate too much.

f) It was too hot outside.

g) My neighbour was completely crazy.

h) This project was very difficult.

i) She was very angry.

j) I had the flu.

k) I was allergic to dogs.

l) The dinner I cooked was disgusting.

5.8   If Only I Had Known

Another common expression used to express regret about something that did or didn't happen in the past is **if only I had known / seen / heard** etc. It is used to indicate that a person did not know something, but if they had known, they would have absolutely done something. **If only** is often used to indicate regret about the past. This can be used with other past tenses, but also in Third Conditional. The form is:

If Only + Pronoun + Had + Past Participle + Pronoun+ Would/Could Have Past Participle

*If Only + Pronoun + Had + Past Participle + Pronoun+ Wouldn't Have Past Participle

* It would be strange to use **couldn't** in these sentences since the speaker is telling us what he /she could have done to stop or fix a situation, not what was impossible.

If only Jane had known her friend was dishonest, **she** never **would have lent** her any money.	But Jane didn't know and she did lend her the money.
If only we **had understood** this car was no good, **we wouldn't have bought** it.	But we did buy the car, and now we have made the mechanic very rich.
If only I had realised eating sugar was so bad for me, **I wouldn't have eaten** so much.	I did know sugar was bad for me. I'm lying to myself so I don't feel so bad.
If only I had known.	Sometimes this is used alone to indicate regret.

5.8.1   Express these situations using *if only*

a) My student needed glasses. She didn't tell me she couldn't see well. I gave her a seat at the back of the classroom. *If only I had known she couldn't see well, I would have given her a seat at the front of the room.*

b) I didn't remember that it was rubbish day and I forgot to take the bins out for the rubbish collector.

c) I forgot to buy coffee when I was at the shops yesterday and this morning I had no coffee to drink.

d) I told Gina my secret and then everyone knew it.

e) Allan didn't prepare for his exams and he failed them.

f) Mary dyed her hair blonde and it looked awful.

g) Lori forgot her sun cream and she got a terrible burn at the beach.

h) I did something stupid.

i) Marcia trusted the wrong people.

j) Oliver left work late and got stuck in a terrible traffic jam.

k) Evan didn't practice piano very well and his music teacher got angry with him.

l) Rory ate too many carrots and turned orange.

m) Diane wasn't a very experienced skier. She tried the black diamond run and broke her leg.

n) I spent all day watching TV and the next day I had a lot of work to do.

o) I didn't receive my friend's email so I didn't write her back.

p) I fed my dog too much food and now he's very fat.

5.9 Third Conditional as Criticism

If Third Conditional can be used to express regret about a past situation, it can also be used to criticise someone for past behaviour. The form is:

If + Pronoun + Past Perfect + Would / Could Have + Past Participle

If + Pronoun + Past Perfect + Wouldn't / Couldn't Have + Past Participle

If you had thought more you would have made better choices.	But you didn't think and you made stupid choices.
If you had read the recipe more carefully the cake you baked wouldn't have been disgusting.	But you didn't read the recipe and the cake is in the rubbish bin.
If you had remembered to feed your poor fish it wouldn't have died.	But you forgot and now the poor thing is dead.

5.9.1 Criticise your friend using Third Conditional

a) Your friend didn't shut her garden gate properly and her dog ran away. *If you had shut the gate properly your dog wouldn't have run away.*

b) She wore uncomfortable shoes and she got painful blisters on her feet.

c) She dated a horrible man who broke her heart.

d) She got a terrible tattoo and her mother got angry.

e) She was lazy in school and failed all her exams.

f) She was driving like an idiot and got into an accident.

g) She woke up late and missed a job interview.

h) She put a red t-shirt in the washing machine with white clothes and everything turned pink.

i) She spent money like a drunken sailor and she had to ask her parents for help.

j) She had a loud party and her neighbours called the police.

k) She didn't do her work properly and her boss sacked her.

l) She lied to her boyfriend and he got angry with her.

m) She promised to help her grandmother and forgot. Her grandmother was disappointed.

n) She drank too much coffee and couldn't sleep at night.

o) She didn't take good care of her teeth and had to do a lot of expensive dental work.

p) She left her car windows open and it rained. Everything got wet.

5.10   The implied "if"

Just like Second Conditional, we can make a Third Conditional sentence without the **if** clause. In these cases, the **if** part of the sentence is understood by the listener, even if it isn't actually said. Often the "implied if" is used when we are hearing a story about something that has happened to another person and we say what we would have done if this thing had happened to us. We use the form:

Pronoun + Would / Could Have + Past Participle

Pronoun + Wouldn't / Couldn't Have + Past Participle

Third Conditional sentence without *if*	Implied part of the sentence
Julia was rude to you in front of all those people? I **would have been so angry.**	*If I had been in your place*, I would have been furious.
Your house was struck by lightning in an electrical storm? **I would have panicked.**	*If that had been me* I would have panicked.
He went to his office Christmas party and got horribly drunk? **I wouldn't have been so stupid.**	*If I had been in his shoes*, I wouldn't have been so stupid.

* *If I had been in (object pronoun) place / If that had been me / If I had been in (object pronoun) shoes* are three common ways of saying what we would do if the same thing happened to us as to other people.

5.10.1 Write sentences using the Implied If

a)   Henry was late arriving at the airport and he missed his flight. *I wouldn't have been so disorganised.*

b)   Your friend was talking on her mobile phone while driving and had an accident.

c)   Alice told her mother-in-law what she really thinks of her.

d)   Ella house was broken into by thieves and she didn't call the police.

e)   Peter spent too much money on his new television.

f)   Jane missed an important appointment because she forgot.

g)   Sam sang on a television talent competition.

h)   Gail climbed Mount Everest.

i)   Rachel was very energetic; she had three jobs and did volunteer work.

j) Kelly forgot to pay her phone bill and her phone was cut off.

k) Donald married a woman he had only known for two weeks.

l) William left a carton of milk in his fridge for three months.

m) Polly stole an expensive jacket from a shop.

n) Evelyn knew what to do in an emergency.

o) Yvonne won the lottery and spent all her money in six months.

p) Frances learned to use a computer at the age of 89.

5.11   Second and Third Conditional Mix

It is common to mix Third and Second Conditional together in the same sentence. This is done when a past possible action has a present possible result. The form is:

If + Pronoun + Past Perfect + Pronoun Would/Could/Might + Infinitive

If + Pronoun + Past Perfect + Pronoun Would Not/ Could Not / Might Not + Infinitive

Third Conditional (Past Condition)	Second Conditional (Present Result)	
If you hadn't helped me	I wouldn't be finished now.	*You helped me and now I am done.*
If we hadn't saved enough money	We wouldn't be on this lovely holiday.	*We saved money and now we're on a holiday.*
If Alice had been more dedicated	she could be a concert pianist now.	*Alice had talent but she didn't practice enough and she's not a famous musician now.*

5.11.1 Match the sentences:

a) If you hadn't woke me up on time	you wouldn't be in this trouble now.
b) If I had won the lottery	you wouldn't be cleaning up a mess right now.
c) If Tessa hadn't invited me to her French class years ago	he would still be living here.
d) If my mum and dad hadn't met	we might still have a misunderstanding.
e) If she hadn't been such a rude person	our dinner wouldn't be in the rubbish.
f) If you had studied more	we wouldn't have any food in the house.
g) If he had paid the rent regularly	she wouldn't be working here.
h) If the police hadn't interviewed the witness	we might be friends right now.
i) If I had read the recipe more carefully	I wouldn't be here right now.
j) If you had been more intelligent	you might have a few friends now.
k) If we hadn't talked clearly about how we felt	I would be late for work right now.
l) If Evelyn hadn't seen that advertisement in the newspaper	I wouldn't be fluent now.

m) If I hadn't gone to the shops last night	I would be sitting on a beach drinking margaritas right now.
n) If you had walked the dog when you were supposed to	you could be a doctor now.
o) If you hadn't been such a disagreeable jerk	the criminal might still be free.

5.12   Third Conditional Sample Sentences

a)   If I'd known what an idiot you were I wouldn't have had anything to do with you. If I had known you were dishonest I wouldn't have invited you to my home. It's a shame, because if you hadn't behaved like this we could have been the best of friends. I think people need friends, but they don't need your type of friend. Maybe if you had been treated better by people in the past you wouldn't be this way now, but you are this way and I don't want anything to do with you.

b)   I got home late from work today and my poor old dog had peed on the floor. It wasn't his fault, it was my fault for being late. If I hadn't been late I could have taken my dog for a walk and he wouldn't have peed on the floor. I was late getting home because my boss (Mr. Stupid Head) asked me to take care of some documents. I took care of the documents, missed my bus and had to wait for the next bus. Maybe I should give my neighbour a key to my house. If my neighbour had had a key she could have let herself in and walked the dog. If I had told my boss that I had to get home because my dog was waiting for me, maybe I could have left early. I'm afraid to tell my boss I have to get home early because of my dog because I suspect my boss is a cat person.

c)   Why on earth did he steal money from his boss? What was he thinking? If he'd been thinking he wouldn't have done such a stupid thing. His boss found out what he'd done and sacked him. Now he's having trouble finding work. If he hadn't been sacked he would have been able to pay his rent. If he had been able to pay his rent he wouldn't have been evicted from his flat. If he hadn't been evicted from his flat he wouldn't be sleeping on his mother's sofa right now. If he had been more intelligent he wouldn't be in this situation.

d)   I'm feeling quite depressed. I had a nice boyfriend called Simon. He was very kind but he was a little bit boring so I left him for a more interesting man called Lance. Lance turned out to be a horrible boyfriend. If I hadn't left Simon, I wouldn't have had my money stolen, or had had all the problems I later had with Lance. I wouldn't have had my heart broken. Now I'm sorry. If I had married Simon I would be happy now. If I hadn't been stupid I would have a different life.

e)   What would you have done if you hadn't studied medicine? Would you have become a chemist? I remember that you were always interested in chemistry. Or would you have studied something else entirely, like journalism? I have always thought that if you hadn't become a doctor, you might have become a ski-instructor in the Alps.

f)   Look at my hair! Oh my God! What was I thinking! This is terrible! If I hadn't decided I needed a new hair-style I wouldn't look like a gigantic blonde mushroom right now. If the hair-stylist hadn't been talking with her co-workers non-stop she might have paid more attention to what was going on with my hair. I have my passport photo tomorrow! If I hadn't been so stupid I wouldn't look like an idiot in my passport for the next ten years.

6. ANSWER KEY:

Zero Conditional

2.1.1

   a) If I don't sleep I am tired all day.

   b) When you talk very loudly you give me a headache.

   c) If I forget my umbrella it rains.

   d) If you are tired go to bed.

   e) When the sun comes out it is quite warm.

   f) If our cat is sick we take him to the veterinarian.

   g) If there is a good film playing on Fridays I usually go with my friends.

   h) If we have time during the summer we usually take a long holiday.

   i) When I have enough money I like to go shopping.

   j) If there is a big storm my dog hides under the bed.

2.1.2   Suggested answers

   a) When it rains, I like to read a book.

   b) When I have enough time, I make a big dinner for my friends.

   c) When I don't have enough time, I order a pizza.

   d) If I don't sleep enough I am in a horrible temper all day.

   e) If a diabetic eats too much sugar, he or she feels sick.

   f) When it is sunny, I read a book in the park.

   g) If she eats too much chocolate, she gets pimples on her chin.

   h) When I eat too much my stomach hurts.

   i) If I forget my umbrella at home, it rains.

   j) When I am late for work, my boss gets angry.

   k) If my dad works too late, my mother is irritated with him.

   l) When the sun is shining I feel happy.

   m) If you leave ice cream in the sun, it melts.

   n) When the sun comes out, the snow melts.

   o) When my alarm clock goes off in the morning, I want to stay bed.

2.1.3

   When you put water in the freezer it turns to ice.

   When the sun goes down at night it gets dark.

   When you take ice out of the freezer, it melts.

   When you add vinegar to baking soda, it makes carbon dioxide.

   When you drink a lot of alcohol, you get drunk and sick.

   When the spring comes the weather turns warm.

   When autumn comes the weather turns cold and the leaves fall off the trees.

   When you bother your teacher, you get into trouble.

   When you don't study for an exam, you fail.

2.1.4 Suggested Answers

a) I like to relax with friends if I have time.

b) It usually rains if I forget my umbrella at home.

c) My best friend gets very angry if you cancel your plans with her.

d) We always go for a walk in the park if the weather is good.

e) I miss the bus in the mornings if I'm unorganised or tired.

f) We can't trust him if he continues to be this way.

g) Danielle can't finish the project if we don't help her.

h) My boss takes us all out for lunch if he's in a good mood.

i) We see a play at the theatre if there is something interesting playing.

j) Helen likes to eat lunch outside if it's a sunny day.

k) My grandparents love to cook big dinners if we all go to their house.

l) Thomas gets a horrible stomach-ache if he eats too much.

m) I sleep late on Sundays if I don't have any plans.

n) They go on an expensive holiday if they save enough money.

o) We go swimming in the sea if the water is warm enough.

2.2.1

a) I don't think you can finish unless I help you.

b) When I get together with my old friends we usually talk about the past.

c) I don't like my aunt. She causes problems whenever she comes to visit.

d) If you don't like your dinner, you don't have to eat it.

e) You pay a lot of money for a hotel unless you get a discount.

f) Helen gets sick when she eats fish.

g) He acts like an idiot whenever he sees a pretty girl.

h) My dog gets scared when there's a thunder storm.

i) There's no possibility of skiing this winter unless we get a lot of snow.

j) If you want to improve you have to practice.

k) I can't help you if you don't tell me what the problem is.

l) Arthur shops like a crazy man whenever he has a little money in his pocket.

m) Water boils when it reaches 100°C.

n) The computer doesn't work if you don't plug it in.

o) The computer doesn't work unless you plug it in.

p) If I don't drink coffee in the morning I'm a zombie all day.

2.3.1

a) If you would prefer to go home we can leave now.

b) She should work harder if she wants the boss to promote her.

c) We had better leave now if we want to arrive in time for the film.

d) I might be able to help you if you tell me what the problem is.

e) Henry must be more serious if he wants people to respect him.

f) If we don't have to finish this project today we might be able to go home early.

g) If you don't have a permit you can't park your car here.

h) If you stop talking I could explain the situation to you.

i) He doesn't need to go to work today. It's Sunday.

j) If you want to lose some weight you must take more exercise.

k) We could finish faster if you would help us.

l) We ought to clean the house if we're having company for dinner this evening.

m) I may visit my friends tonight if I have time.

n) Shawn really has to be more organised if he is going to succeed.

o) Gerald can help me if I need any assistance.

2.4.1

a) If we are free in the evenings then we like to go out with our friends.

b) If you drink too much then you get drunk.

c) If you watch too much television then you get a headache.

d) If the baby makes a mess then I clean it up.

e) If I have a lot of work to do then I make a list to help myself get organised.

f) If Julia gets angry then she embarrasses herself by shouting.

g) I'm allergic to fish. If I eat fish then I have to go to hospital.

h) If the birds are singing very loudly in the morning then I can't sleep.

i) If Gabriel has enough money then he can buy a new car.

j) It's cold outside. If you want to go for a walk then you need to take a jacket.

k) If Maria gets a headache then she takes an aspirin.

l) If you eat all that ice-cream then you will get a stomach-ache.

m) If you practice piano every day then you improve.

n) If you don't brush your teeth then you get cavities.

o) If Polly leaves work early then the boss gets angry.

2.4.2 Suggested Answers

a) If David wants to go to Tokyo then he must/ has to / should / had better learn Japanese.

b) If we want to be on time for our class then we have to / should hurry.

c) If you don't want to get sick then you need to eat your vegetables.

d) If Layla wants to lose a few kilos then she mustn't eat so much candy.

e) If Paul needs money then he could ask me.

f) If you want people to respect you then you have to act like an adult.

g) If we don't have any homework tonight then we might go out.

h) If you don't know what to do then you should ask someone for help.

i) If you want to improve your English then you have to practice daily.

j) If you feel sick then you might have to go to the doctor.

k) If he wants to finish this project on time then he had better get organised.

l) If Jack wants to catch the train at six o'clock tomorrow morning then he should go to bed early.

m) If we have time then we could go to a show this evening.

n) If Mark takes the time to cook a lovely dinner then we have to eat it.

o) If Frances is interested in art then she should take some classes.

2.5.1 Suggested Answers

a) My tooth hurts.   If your tooth hurts, (then) go to the dentist.

b) If you're tired, (then) go to bed.

c) If you're fat (then) don't eat so many sweets.

d) If your hair is too long (then) get it cut.

e) If your fingernails don't look nice (then) get a manicure.

f) If your flat is a mess (then) clean it.

g) If your stomach hurts (then) see a doctor.

h) If your grades aren't good (then) study more.

i) If you have no friends (then) learn to be nicer.

j) If you're a terrible dancer (then) take lessons.

k) If you're hungry (then) eat.

l) If your clothes are dirty (then) wash them.

m) If you have no money (then) get a job.

n) If you have a lot of work to do (then) stop complaining and do it.

o) If you're late for work (then) hurry!

p) If your car broke down (then) call a mechanic.

2.5.2 Suggested Answers

a) Finding friends   If you want to find friends you have to go out and meet people.

b) If you have a lot of stress you should learn to breathe slowly and deeply.

c) If you need to be more organised you should make lists and plan your day carefully.

d) If you want to stay fit you should exercise each day.

e) If you want to be more relaxed you should find some enjoyable activities.

f) If you need more free time you can always organise your day differently.

g) If you have to deal with difficult people it's always good to smile and think pleasant thoughts.

h) If you feel tired and have no energy you might want to visit your doctor.

i) If you don't have enough money you can keep careful track of where you spend money to see what you can eliminate.

j) If you want to find love you have to first love yourself.

k) If you're unhappy with your life you can make changes.

l) If you have problems at work you can learn stress-reducing exercises.

m) If you feel sick all the time you must see a doctor.

n) If you don't know how to cook you can find excellent tutorials and recipes on the internet.

o) If you don't know where to shop you should ask people for advice.

p) If you want to find something interesting to do you could always check the internet to see what's new.

2.6.1

    a) Don't talk to me when I'm talking on the phone.

    b) My father gets angry if I wake him up.

    c) Hilary never wears her glasses unless she's driving.

    d) I never wear elegant clothes unless I'm going to a party.

    e) Joseph sends me a postcard whenever he's travelling.

    f) They are never happy unless they are working.

    g) I won't speak to her about important things when she's drinking.

    h) Pamela can't hear you if you're speaking so quietly.

    i) I'm not drinking that coffee if Randall made it.

    j) Melissa stays up late every night unless she's feeling tired.

    k) I prefer not to answer the phone when I'm working.

    l) Close the windows if it's raining.

    m) If you're feeling hungry then make yourself a sandwich.

    n) Go to the doctor if you're feeling sick.

    o) Answer the phone if it's ringing.

First Conditional

3.1.1   Match the sentences

    a) If you don't understand the homework I'll help you.

    b) If Jack hears this story he will be very angry.

    c) If you make coffee for yourself I'll drink some too.

    d) If it rains we won't be able to go to the seaside.

    e) If you work hard you will be successful.

    f) If she continues to come to work late the boss will fire her.

    g) If we don't hurry up we will be late for our meeting.

    h) If you can't help me I will find someone else who can.

    i) If I have nothing to do this evening I'll watch TV.

    j) If we see something nice in the shops we'll buy it.

    k) If the weather is good we'll go on a picnic tomorrow.

    l) If we can find a cheap flight we'll go to Morocco on our holiday.

    m) If there's a good film playing we'll go to the cinema tomorrow.

    n) If you don't stop talking I'll be very angry with you.

    o) If he thinks he can do whatever he wants with no consequences he will be very surprised.

3.1.2   Suggested Answers

    a) I'd like to go on a picnic today but if it rains I'll stay home.

    b) If I have time I will help you.

    c) If you drink ten beers you will get drunk.

    d) I'm very angry at him. When I see him I will kill him.

    e) If you call me again I will call the police.

f) I can see you are angry with John. When I see him I will tell him.

g) If we don't have any bottled water I will drink tap water.

h) If we go out for dinner I will pay.

i) If I have enough money I will take a holiday.

j) If they call us to go out with them we won't go.

k) When I finish school I will be a doctor.

l) If you don't tell me the truth I will be very disappointed in you.

m) When he calls me I will tell him you said hello.

n) When my boss comes back I will be in trouble.

o) If I forget my umbrella it will rain.

3.1.3

If they have an adventure film I won't go because I hate adventure films. / And if there is a romantic film I definitely won't go because I can't stand romantic films. /
But if there is a thriller, I will go because I like thrillers. / But if the thriller is starring Peter Wonderful, I won't go because I don't like Peter Wonderful. / But if there is a thriller, and that thriller doesn't have Peter Wonderful, I will certainly go. If the popcorn is cold I won't go. / If ticket is too expensive, I won't go. Then again, if the ticket is not very expensive, I won't go because it probably means the cinema is old.
/ If the cinema is too old , I won't go./ If the cinema is new it will be too busy and I don't like a cinema with a lot of people.

3.1.4   Suggested Answers

a) I won't speak to you if you are rude to me.

b) She will be very happy when she hears the news.

c) My grandmother will come and visit us if she feels better.

d) I'll go for a pizza with my friends if my mum lets me.

e) We'll watch a movie later if we finish our work.

f) I'll cook dinner if you wash the dishes.

g) Harry will clean the house if you pay him.

h) I'll buy you a new sweater if you want one.

i) Kate will call you when she has time.

j) They won't be happy when they hear what you've done.

k) Gavin will go to Paris if he can save the money.

l) Polly won't wear those shoes if it's raining.

m) We won't go skiing this winter if there is no snow.

n) David will be late coming home this evening if his boss makes him stay.

o) Rachel will do the shopping if I give her some money.

p) James will go to university if he gets good grades.

3.2.1

    a) We won't have fun at the party ____unless____ Peter comes too.

    b) Edward will tell us the story as soon as he comes home.

    c) Sam will be very happy when he hears the good news.

    d) If she has enough money in her budget our boss will take us out for an expensive lunch.

    e) I will be very angry if she's rude to me again.

    f) Unless the situation improves we will have to find a new apartment.

    g) Clean your room as soon as you can.

    h) I think I will improve my French if I practice a lot.

    i) I will be very angry if you tell anyone.

    j) I won't be able to do my report if the computer doesn't work.

    k) They will call us from the airport as soon as their plane lands in London.

    l) My dog won't go outside unless I go out with him.

    m) You will get very sick unless you stop smoking.

    n) I won't go to the doctor unless I feel very sick.

    o) They'll buy a new house as soon as they save the money.

    p) William won't talk about his problems unless you ask him directly.

3.3.1   Match the sentences

    a) If she discovers what you've done she is going to kill you.

    b) William is going to be exhausted if he continues to work so hard.

    c) I'm not going to speak with you again if you behave so badly.

    d) You're going to be sick if you drink all that vodka.

    e) I'm going to buy a new tablet as soon as I save enough money.

    f) When Mum and Dad see this mess they're going to be very angry.

    g) They're not going to buy a house unless they have the money.

    h) I'm going to visit Grandmother if she's feeling better.

    i) Gina is going to start dancing again when her leg feels better.

    j) Anna isn't going to invite him to her party unless he apologises for his rudeness.

    k) I'm going to finish reading this book as soon as you stop interrupting me.

    l) You're not going to be on time for work if you continue to waste time doing stupid things.

    m) The television isn't going to work unless you plug it in to the electrical socket.

    n) If I have time I'm going to make you a lovely breakfast.

    o) Lana is going to call her parents as soon as she gets home.

3.4.1 Suggested Answers

    a) If we get to the restaurant before it closes then we will order dinner.

    b) If you forgot your keys in the car then we will be in trouble.

    c) If the library is open then I'll get some books for us to read.

    d) If the exam is on Tuesday then I will start studying now.

    e) If you're tired then I'll make the bed for you.

    f) It's Sunday and we have time to relax. If you feel like it then we will go out.

g) If our neighbour has another loud party tonight then I will call the police.

h) If you don't have time to wash the dishes then I will do it for you.

i) If Diana doesn't want to come to our party then she isn't going to come.

j) If it's hot again tomorrow then I'll turn on the air conditioning.

k) If Jack keeps complaining about stupid things then I am going to tell him to shut up.

l) If Theo isn't more polite to me then I'm going to walk away.

m) If Polly doesn't give me back the money I lent her then I'll be very cross with her.

n) It's very cold today. If you wear that light summer dress then you'll be cold all day.

o) Let's clean the house together. If you wash the floors then I'll do the laundry.

p) If I get to the post office before it closes then I'll send the letter.

3.5.1

a) If you   can't help me   I'll call someone else.

b) I'll tell you when I have to go.

c) I really must study if I'm going to pass that exam.

d) You'd better go to the post office now or you won't be able to pick up your mail.

e) Ryan must be more responsible or his boss won't give him the promotion.

f) I ought to walk the dog now or he'll start to whine and bark.

g) I should do the laundry or we won't have any clean clothes to wear.

h) As soon as I can talk for a few minutes I will phone you.

i) If you must take the ten o'clock train you'll have to leave now.

j) If you don't have to go to work today then I'll stay home too.

k) If you could carry the books then I'll carry the clothes.

l) Unless you have to go right now I'll start cooking dinner.

m) You had better tell me the truth or I'm going to be very upset with you.

n) You should eat now or you'll be very hungry later on.

o) We ought to prepare our picnic or we won't have anything to eat.

p) She has to apologise or Jane won't forgive her.

3.6.1   Suggested Answers

a) Sit down or __I'll get angry_____.

b) Sit down and I'll help you.

c) Tell the truth or you'll get it trouble.

d) Tell the truth and you won't get in trouble.

e) Come here or I'll be angry.

f) Drink your juice and I'll make you breakfast.

g) Don't be stupid or your mum will get angry.

h) Finish your homework and we'll go to a movie.

i) Finish your homework or we won't go to a movie.

j) Go to bed or you'll be tired tomorrow.

k) Don't make a mess in here or your mum and dad will explode.

l) We're going on a trip. Go put petrol in the car and I'll pack the clothes.

m) Make lunch and I'll wash the dishes.

n) Pack the picnic food and I'll get the plates and cutlery.

o) It's raining. Close the windows or everything will get wet.

p) Don't jump on the furniture or you'll fall off and hurt yourself.

3.7.1 Suggested Answers

a) If the baby is finally sleeping we won't make any noise.

b) If the dog is jumping around at the door I'll take him out for a walk.

c) If you're making more coffee I'll have a cup too.

d) If she's cleaning the house I won't help her.

e) If Annie is cooking we'll all have a lovely dinner.

f) If Tom is working tomorrow he won't be able to come out with us.

g) If the teacher is getting angry I won't ask for help.

h) If you're having lunch I'll join you.

i) If you're driving your car to work today I'll come with you.

j) If he's losing all his money at the casinos he'll be in big trouble with his wife.

k) If there's anything good playing at the cinema we'll go.

l) If it's raining today we won't have a picnic.

m) If Oliver is playing football tonight we'll go and watch him.

n) If Edward is being disrespectful I'll tell him what a jerk he is.

o) If Daniel is taking a shower now I won't flush the toilet.

p) If the weather is getting colder we won't go to the beach.

3.8.1

a) Freddy will be hungry if you haven't finished cooking dinner yet.

b) The baby will be asleep if we've been quiet enough.

c) The car won't start if you haven't bothered to fill it with petrol.

d) If we've run out of milk I'll go to the shops and buy some.

e) I won't watch the film on television if it has already started.

f) If you have done your homework by seven o'clock we can catch a film at the cinema.

g) If Gordon has arrived by twelve o'clock I'll make him some lunch.

h) If the post office has closed by the time we arrive I won't be able to send this stupid letter.

i) If she hasn't finished cleaning her room she won't be able to hang out with her friends.

j) If my brother hasn't arrived home by midnight our parents will be very worried about him.

k) If the dog hasn't been fed yet he'll jump up and down and whine and bark.

l) If you've finished drinking your water I'll pour you another glass.

m) If we've saved enough money we'll go on a nice holiday.

n) He will be in a terrible temper all day if he hasn't had a good night's sleep.

o) If I have been rude to Martha I will apologise to her.

3.9.1 Suggested Answers

a) If you buy new clothes you won't have enough money to pay your rent.

b) If you spend too much money you have a lot of problems.

c) If I'm late for work the boss will kill me. / As soon as I arrive at work the boss will kill me

d) If Alice isn't more intelligent she'll lose her next job, too. / If you're late for work you lose your job.

e) If you don't exercise you can't lose weight. If you want to lose weight you are going to have to exercise.

f) You have to exercise if you want to lose weight.

g) If you continue drinking you're going to be sorry tomorrow.

h) If you don't learn to brush your teeth you will have serious dental problems. / As soon as the dentist sees your mouth he's going to start to cry.

i) If you don't take good care of your dental health you have problems with your teeth.

j) If you don't wear a sweater you'll be cold all day.

k) If there's a good film playing we will go and see it.

l) If you eat that fruit salad you'll have a terrible allergic reaction.

m) If you have diabetes you mustn't eat sugary snacks.

n) If Carla continues being rude to people she won't have any friends.

o) If I'm hungry later on I will eat something.

p) If my friends see my messy house they'll be horrified.

Second Conditional

4.1.1 Suggested answers

a) Win the lottery (for example... If I won the lottery I would take a very long holiday.)

b) If I found a lot of money I would have a great holiday.

c) If I dated a famous person I would have my picture taken all the time.

d) If I met the Prime Minister I'd tell him what an idiot he is.

e) If I built a time machine I would go back in time and meet famous people.

f) If I were a genius I would stop world hunger.

g) If I had a new car I wouldn't take the bus anymore.

h) If I were very beautiful / handsome I'd be a movie star.

i) If I were a very good student I'd speak ten languages.

j) If I were a politician I'd be an idiot too.

k) If I traveled at the speed of light I'd never be late for work again.

l) If I became invisible I would go to the cinema and not pay.

m) If I had enough time I would be more organised.

n) If I knew the secrets of the universe I wouldn't tell them to anyone.

o) If I met an alien I would buy him a beer.

p) If I had a holiday beach house I would have a lot of friends.

4.1.2

If I weren't feeling sick I would be better. / If I had some aspirin, my head wouldn't hurt so much. / If my nose wasn't stuffed up I would breathe better. / If could breathe better I would be able to sleep all night. / If I could sleep I wouldn't feel so tired. / And if I weren't so tired I would feel better. / If I had a better jacket I would be warmer. / And if I were warmer I probably wouldn't have a cold at all. / If I were more interesting people would stay and talk to me. / If I had time I would stay longer but I have an appointment with my dentist!

4.1.3   Suggested answers

a) Jim would start to cry if you took away his beer.

b) My neighbour would be very angry if I had an all-night party.

c) I would shop in all the most expensive places if I won the lottery.

d) We would travel the world if we had the time or money.

e) Frieda would have more friends if she weren't so rude.

f) Olivia wouldn't be so unorganised if she took the time to plan her day.

g) Mr. and Mrs. Jones would be happier if they went out more and visited with friends.

h) We wouldn't be angry if you just told us the truth.

i) Ronald would go skiing every weekend if he could.

j) I would be more motivated if I had a more interesting job.

k) William would be in better physical condition if he weren't so lazy.

l) My team would win more games if they had more training.

m) The dog wouldn't bark and jump around so much if you took him for a walk.

n) He would sleep better at night if he didn't drink so much coffee.

o) I would run away screaming and shouting if I saw my teacher without her make-up on.

p) You would be more successful if you tried harder.

4.2.1   Suggested answers

a) If I were rich I would share with everyone except my boss.

b) If I were younger I would go back to school.

c) If I were old I would retire and work in my garden.

d) If I were an alien from another planet I would look at Earth, get scared and go home.

e) If I were more organised I would get things done on time.

f) If I were in better physical condition I would run a marathon.

g) If I were angry with someone I would tell them.

h) If I were feeling better I would go out with you.

i) If I were a movie star I would make fantastic films.

j) If I were about to buy a new car I would read a lot about the cars that are available.

k) If I were living in Paris I would eat brioche every day.

l) If I were in your situation I would manage it better than you.

m) If I were any animal in the world I would be an elephant.

n) If I were a super hero I would attack politicians.

o) If I were a politician I would be afraid of super-heroes.

4.3.1

a) My stomach really hurts. If I were you I would see a doctor.

b) If I were him I would make better choices.

c) If I were her I would be more honest.

d) If I were you I would stop using the internet at work.

e) If I were you I wouldn't eat so much cake.

f) If I were them I would be more respectful.

g) If I were him I would clean my house.

h) If I were her I would eat vegetables.

i) If I were Shannon I would try to get a better job.

j) If I were him I would eat a better diet.

k) If I were you I would go to bed early.

l) If I were her I wouldn't drink coffee at night.

m) If I were him I would get some exercise.

n) If I were you I would go to the dentist.

o) If I were you I would find a hobby.

p) If I were Jane I would break up with him.

4.4.1

a) Rachel is asking you what you would do if you were in her position. *What would you do if you were me?*

b) If I were him I would.....

c) If I were him I would...

d) If I were you two I would ...

e) If I were you I would...

f) If I were her I would...

g) If I were him I would...

h) If I were him I would....

i) If I were him I would....

j) If I were you I would...

k) If I were her I would...

l) What would you do if you were me?

m) What would you do if you were her?

n) What would you do if you were them?

o) What would you do if you were them?

p) What would you do if you were her/him?

4.5.1   Suggested answers

a) What would you do if you were a great singer? *I would give concerts all over the world.*

b) I would have a huge party.

c) I would invite him over to my house for dinner.

d) I would travel to India.

e) I would eat a cheeseburger and a chocolate milkshake.

f) I would be a journalist.

g) I would be more positive and more active.

h) I would take a lot of pictures.

i) I would still probably take the bus.

j) I would learn to speak ten languages.

k) I would sack myself.

l) It would be invisibility.

m) I would punch him in the nose and then tell her.

n) If I knew a secret about someone I didn't like, I wouldn't say anything.

o) If I had unlimited time and unlimited money I would do everything.

p) If I had a time machine I would go back in time and meet Marie Curie.

4.6.1   Match the sentences:

a) If I had more money I could buy whatever I wanted.

b) If you were nicer to people you could have more friends.

c) If I were in better physical shape I could run a marathon.

d) I could concentrate on this problem better if you stopped talking so loudly.

e) If my house were more organised I could find my keys and bag more easily.

f) If she dressed more professionally she could find a better job.

g) If they didn't spend money like drunken sailors they could have more in the bank.

h) If you worked less you could spend more time with your family.

i) If we woke up earlier in the morning we could get more done during the day.

j) If you didn't turn the television up so loud the baby could sleep.

k) If the weather was nicer we could go for a walk today.

l) We could go to London if we found a cheap flight.

m) Evan could do better in school if he studied harder.

n) We could change our lives if we really wanted to.

o) George could have a girlfriend if he weren't so socially awkward.

4.7.1   Suggested Answers

a) If the TV repairman came over to fix our television, we might be able to watch the football match.

b) If you did all your homework before six o'clock you might have some free time

c) If she put more effort into her work she might not have so many problems.

d) If you didn't eat so quickly your stomach might not hurt so much.

e) If went out with your friends more often you might feel better.

f) If you got a hair-cut you might look nicer.

g) If you took an aspirin you might feel better.

h) If I told her how I feel she might be angry with me.

i) If he didn't drink so much he might be healthier.

j) If we took more care with the garden it might look better.

k) If you didn't spend all your money the first day you got paid you might have more.

l) If Larry was kinder and more polite to people he might not be so unpopular.

m) If he didn't smoke so much he might be able to walk.

n) If he spent less time on the internet he might have a real life.

o) If he worked harder he might be more successful.

p) If he met normal women he might not be so miserable.

4.8.1 Suggested Answers

a) If I could have one super power I would fly.

b) If I could go anywhere in the world I would go to Tibet.

c) If I could meet anyone from history I would meet Queen Elizabeth I.

d) If we could buy anything we wanted we would buy a big house.

e) If I could take a holiday I would go to Thailand.

f) If I could find my keys I would be able to go to work.

g) If she could walk faster she wouldn't be behind us all the time.

h) If I could find more time I would relax with friends more.

i) If I could draw really well I would be an artist.

j) If I could play any sport I would play football.

k) If I could cook very well I would make dinner for all my friends.

l) If I could have any job in the world I would be a surgeon.

m) If I could hack into any website I would make a lot of trouble for my bank.

n) If we could take the whole summer off and not work we would go to the beach every day.

o) If we could stop arguing and fighting we would see that we love each other.

p) If I could have a conversation with my dog I would ask him why he ate my new shoes.

4.9.1

a) It's three o'clock in the morning and I can't sleep. If it weren't for my noisy neighbours *I would be sleeping right now.*

b) If it weren't for my parents I would be skiing right now.

c) If it weren't for being late we would be watching the film.

d) If it weren't for me I would be cooking dinner.

e) If it weren't for his boss he would be going out with his friends.

f) If it weren't for the job market she would be working as an architect.

g) If it weren't for the accident he would be driving his car.

h) If they weren't full we would be staying in this hotel.

i) If it weren't for his cold he would be feeling better.

j) If my leg weren't broken I would be training for the marathon.

k) If it weren't for that crazy dog we would be eating steak.

l) If he weren't such an idiot he would be dating a supermodel.

m) If I weren't such a clumsy person my phone would be working.

n) If it weren't flat he would be riding his bike.

o) If it weren't for that exam she would be relaxing in front of the TV.

p) If I weren't so greedy my tooth wouldn't be hurting.

4.10.1

b) Did you see how much Kelly eats? Incredible! I would be very fat!

c) You ran 25 km today? I would be exhausted!

d) Hilary didn't get the promotion her boss promised her after all the work she did. I would be so angry!

e) Allen's daughter won the music competition. I would be so proud!

f) Nigel drank fifteen glasses of beer last night. I would have a huge headache.

g) You haven't slept properly in a week? I would be so tired!

h) His brother is the best at everything and Larry is a bit of a loser. I would be so envious.

i) I can't understand Bob. He can never find anything and he's always late. I would be more organised.

j) Sandra charges three dollars an hour to clean houses. I would ask for more money.

k) Charlie is a brilliant chef. His cakes are fantastic. I would burn everything.

k) Virginia has been complaining for weeks that her tooth hurts her. I would go to the dentist.

m) Your co-worker took your idea and said it was his? I would complain to the boss.

n) David bought an expensive new television and after one week it was broken. I would take it back the shop.

n) Annie won't return your phone calls? I would go over to her house and ask her what the problem is.

o) No one came to Nancy's birthday party. I would cry.

4.11.1

a) Your friend is talking about how she wishes she could take a trip around the world. (go) Where *would you go?*

b) Who would you take?

c) What kind of pet would you get?

d) Where would you live?

e) How would you spend the money?

f) What would you do?

g) Which instrument would you play?

h) What would you do?

i) How many children would you have?

j) What would you say to her?

k) How would we pay for it?

l) Who would you meet?

m) What would you study?

n) What would you sell?

o) How would you explain yourself?

p) How would you manage?

4.12.1

a) I wish my job were great.

b) I wish the weather were better.

c) We wish we weren't so busy.

d) He wishes he had a girlfriend.

e) I wish this weren't so complicated.

f) I wish I didn't eat so much.

g) I wish it weren't so hot out.

h) I wish my neighbour weren't so crazy.

i) I wish the project weren't so difficult.

j) I wish she weren't so angry.

k) They wish they had a better apartment.

l) I wish I didn't have the flu.

m) I wish I weren't allergic to dogs.

n) I wish my dinner were better.

o) I wish I weren't horrible at Maths.

THIRD CONDITIONAL

5.1.1

My brother told my mum I was smoking cigarettes so I hit him. If my brother hadn't told on my I wouldn't have hit him.

b) If I hadn't drunk so much coffee I wouldn't have felt sick.

c) If I hadn't dropped my phone it wouldn't have got broken.

d) If I hadn't left my book outside it wouldn't have been ruined.

e) If I had brushed my teeth carefully I wouldn't have had cavities.

f) If I hadn't spilled coffee on my shirt it wouldn't have been stained.

0 If George hadn't forgotten to call me I wouldn't have been angry.

h) If she hadn't missed the bus she wouldn't have been late for work.

i) If the bank hadn't been closed I would have taken out money.

j) If I had finished my work I would have gone out with my friends.

k) If I hadn't left the milk on the table it wouldn't have gone bad.

l) If I hadn't told her my real opinion she wouldn't have got angry with me.

m) If Bill hadn't forgotten to pay his electric bill his electricity would not have been turned off.

n) If Sally hadn't left her handbag on the bus someone wouldn't have stolen her money and ID.

0 If I hadn't met Alex I wouldn't have become a doctor.

p) If I hadn't been late coming home I wouldn't have missed your call.

q) If I had been paying attention I wouldn't have got into an accident.

r) If Greg hadn't told a lie he wouldn't have got into trouble.

s) If Zoe hadn't forgotten to feed her fish it wouldn't have died.

5.1.2

a) If I had known the car was no good I wouldn't have bought it.

b) If I had known my friends were going to come over I would have gone shopping. / If my friends had called first I would have gone shopping.

c) If I hadn't bought those clothes I would have been able to pay my rent.

d) If I hadn't eaten that food I wouldn't have got sick.

e) If I hadn't told Mr. Big Mouth my secret it wouldn't have become public knowledge.

f) If I hadn't forgotten my mother's birthday she wouldn't have been angry with me.

g) If she hadn't broke the law she wouldn't have had legal problems.

h) If he hadn't married the wrong woman he would have been happier.

i) If I hadn't been to university I wouldn't have learned some interesting things.

j) If I hadn't been talking on the phone I would have noticed that my dinner was burning. / If I had been paying attention my dinner wouldn't have burned.

k) If I hadn't got that terrible haircut I wouldn't have looked like such an idiot for school photos.

l) If I hadn't studied for that exam I wouldn't have passed.

m) If my friends had studied for that exam they would have passed.

n) If I hadn't stayed up late I wouldn't have been late for work. / If I hadn't watched that film I would have been on time for work.

o) If I had known he was a vegetarian I would have made tofu.

5.1.3

If I hadn't been sending a message I wouldn't have got into an accident.

If I hadn't hit the fire hydrant the streets wouldn't have been flooded with water.

If I hadn't shouted at the policeman I wouldn't have been arrested.

If I had had the money I wouldn't have spent the night in jail.

If I hadn't spent the night in jail I wouldn't have been late for work the next morning.

If I hadn't been late for work I wouldn't have been fired.

If I hadn't been fired I would have been able to pay my rent.

If I had been able to pay my rent I wouldn't have been thrown out of my apartment.

5.2.1   Suggested Answers

a) I would have helped you if I had known you were in trouble.

b) I wouldn't have said such a stupid thing if I had known the whole situation.

c) He would have tried harder if he had known his boss was watching him.

d) We would have slept better if the neighbours hadn't had a big huge party.

e) Sandra wouldn't have missed the bus if she had woken up earlier.

f) Peter would have won the competition if Kevin hadn't cheated.

g) Ella would have been able to speak German better if she had lived in Germany.

h) They wouldn't have been so angry with you if you hadn't been such an ass.

i) I wouldn't have had a headache if I hadn't drunk so much.

j) Luke wouldn't have had legal problems if he hadn't broken the law.

k) I wouldn't have locked my keys inside my car if I had paid attention.

l) We wouldn't have been late for the film if we'd left on time.

m) George would have had better luck with girls if he hadn't been so creepy.

n) Henry would have known the truth if he had asked me.

o) Jane would have had more friends at school if she hadn't been so rude.

5.3.1

a) If we'd had more time in London we could have visited the museums.

b) If I had worked harder when I was in school I could have become a doctor.

c) You could have arrived home a lot faster if you had taken the bus instead of walked.

d) If they had been more honest with each other they could have had a better marriage.

e) If I'd taken better care of my teeth I could have avoided an expensive trip to the dentist.

f) If you hadn't been busy on Saturday you could have come to my birthday party.

g) Jerry could have been chosen for the basketball team if he hadn't hurt his leg.

h) If I hadn't been obligated to go to my aunt's house for dinner I could have come to your party.

i) If the police had been given the information they could have caught the criminal.

j) Laura could have come to visit us for a week if she hadn't been so busy with work.

k) If I had known your car was being repaired I could have given you a lift home.

l) If our company had signed that contract we all could have received a fantastic pay rise.

m) We could have gone out on Friday night if we hadn't been so tired.

n) If he'd had flour and eggs he could have made a cake.

o) We could have got a dog if my husband hadn't been allergic to animals.

5.4.1

a) I wasn't paying attention and I lost my wallet on the bus. If I had been paying attention I might not have lost my wallet on the bus.

b) If I hadn't forgotten to take my car to the mechanic it might not have needed repairs.

c) If Eddie had eaten properly he might not have got sick.

d) If Julia hadn't taken so many pain pills they might still work for her.

e) If I hadn't left my window open the thieves might not have come in and I might be watching TV right now instead of writing a grammar book.

f) If Harold hadn't gone to that restaurant he might not have met his future wife.

g) If I hadn't read that book I might not have become an archaeologist.

h) If Lila had listened to the doctor her foot might have healed faster.

i) If he'd never taken that yoga class he might not have found his dream job.

j) If the police hadn't found that clue the criminal might not have been caught.

k) If Bob hadn't helped that man he might not have become an EMT.

l) If I hadn't gone for a walk I might never have found that house.

m) If I hadn't been talking to my aunt I might never have heard that story about my grandmother.

n) If I hadn't gone into that restaurant I might not have found a new favourite place.

o) If we hadn't learned the truth we might not have defended our friend.

p) If Mary hadn't watched that cooking show she might not have become a chef.

5.5.1

a) I was sleeping and I missed the television show. If I hadn't been sleeping I wouldn't have missed the TV show.

b) If I hadn't been studying I could have gone to the party.

c) If it hadn't been snowing the skiing wouldn't have been so great.

d) If we hadn't been arguing so loudly we would have understood each other.

e) If she hadn't been listening to her music she would have heard the phone ring.

f) If she hadn't been recovering from the flu she would / could have gone camping.

g) If Oliver hadn't been trying so hard his teacher wouldn't have given him extra points.

h) If Jen hadn't been talking constantly other people could have participated in the conversation.

i) If it hadn't been raining so hard the garden wouldn't have been flooded with water.

j) If Marlene hadn't been learning Mandarin she wouldn't have made new friends.

k) If I hadn't been working I could / would have gone home early.

l) If she hadn't been feeling anxious she could / would have slept at night.

m) If he hadn't been drinking he wouldn't have got into an accident.

n) If I hadn't been staying with my friends I wouldn't have learned how to cook.

o) If Dad hadn't been cooking dinner he could / would have helped me with my homework.

p) If Ella hadn't been looking at an old photo she wouldn't have seen something strange.

5.6.1

a) You lost your keys and had to pay a lot of money to get someone to open your door. If I hadn't lost my keys I wouldn't have had to pay a lot of money to get someone to open the door.

b) If I had known he was having medical problems I would have helped him.

c) If I hadn't had to go to that birthday party I could have gone to the cinema.

d) If I hadn't bought those shoes I wouldn't have been broke.

e) If I had known her size I wouldn't have bought the wrong shirt.

f) If I hadn't eaten something bad I wouldn't have got sick.

g) If I hadn't been such a big-mouth my friend wouldn't have been angry with me.

h) If I hadn't been working I could /would have gone to the theatre with my friends.

i) If I had known the electricity had gone out I could have fixed the fuse and my food wouldn't have spoiled.

j) If my tire hadn't got a puncture I could have gone for a bike ride on Saturday.

k) If I had known he was allergic to fish I wouldn't have made salmon for dinner.

l) If I had known the papers were important I wouldn't have thrown them out.

m) If I hadn't got drunk I wouldn't have lost my job.

n) If my phone hadn't fallen on the floor I wouldn't have had to buy another one.

o) If I hadn't drunk the coffee I wouldn't have burned my mouth.

p) If I hadn't stayed up and watched that film I wouldn't have been tired the next day.

5.7.1

a) I wish my job hadn't been terrible.

b) I wish the weather hadn't been horrible.

c) We wish we hadn't been very busy.

d) I wish this hadn't been so complicated.

e) I wish I hadn't eaten so much.

f) I wish it hadn't been so hot outside.

g) I wish my neighbour hadn't been so crazy.

h) I wish the project hadn't been so difficult.

i) I wish she hadn't been so angry.

j) I wish I hadn't had the flu.

k) I wish I hadn't been allergic to dogs.

l) I wish the dinner I cooked hadn't been disgusting.

5.8.1

a) My student needed glasses. She didn't tell me she couldn't see well. I gave her a seat at the back of the classroom. *If only I had known she couldn't see well, I would have given her a seat at the front of the room.*

b) If only I had remembered to take out the rubbish bins.

c) If only I had bought coffee I wouldn't have been so unhappy this morning.

d) If only I hadn't told Big Mouth Gina my secret everyone else wouldn't have known it too.

e) If only Allen had prepared for his exams he wouldn't have failed.

f) If only Mary hadn't dyed her hair blonde she wouldn't have looked so ridiculous.

g) If only Lori hadn't forgotten her sun cream she wouldn't have got such a horrible burn.

h) If only I hadn't done something stupid.

i) If only Marcia hadn't trusted the wrong people.

j) If only Oliver hadn't left work late he wouldn't have got stuck in a traffic jam.

k) If only Evan had practiced more his teacher wouldn't have been angry with him.

l) If only Rory hadn't eaten so many carrots he wouldn't have turned orange.

m) If only Diane hadn't tried that black diamond run she wouldn't have broken her leg.

n) If only I hadn't spent all day watching TV I wouldn't have been so busy the next day.

o) If only I had received my friend's email I would have written her back.

p) If only I hadn't overfed my dog he wouldn't have looked like a sausage.

5.9.1

a) Your friend didn't shut her garden gate properly and her dog ran away. *If you had shut the gate properly your dog wouldn't have run away.*

b) If you hadn't worn such stupid shoes you wouldn't have got blisters.

c) If you hadn't dated such a jerk you wouldn't have had your heart broken.

d) If you hadn't got that ugly tattoo your mother wouldn't have got angry.

e) If you hadn't been so lazy you wouldn't have failed all your exams.

f) If you hadn't been driving like an idiot you wouldn't have got into an accident.

g) If you hadn't woken up late you wouldn't have missed that job interview.

h) If you hadn't put a red shirt in the wash everything wouldn't have turned pink.

i) If you hadn't spent money like a drunken sailor you wouldn't have had to ask your parents for help.

j) If you hadn't had a loud party your neighbours wouldn't have called the police.

k) If you had done your work properly your boss wouldn't have sacked you.

l) If you hadn't lied to your boyfriend he wouldn't have got angry with you.

m) If you had helped your granny she wouldn't have been disappointed.

n) If you hadn't drunk so much coffee you would have slept properly.

o) If you had taken good care of your teeth you wouldn't have had to spend money at the dentist.

p) If you hadn't left your car windows open you wouldn't have had a wet car.

5.10.1

a) Henry was late arriving at the airport and he missed his flight. *I wouldn't have been so disorganised.*

b) I wouldn't have used my phone while driving.

c) I wouldn't have been so honest.

d) I would have called the police.

e) I would probably have spent even more money. I love televisions.

f) I wouldn't have forgotten an appointment.

g) I wouldn't have been so brave.

h) I wouldn't have been so adventurous.

i) I wouldn't have been able to manage such a schedule.

j) I wouldn't have forgotten to pay my bill.

k) I wouldn't have married someone I had just met.

l) I would have thrown the milk into the bin.

m) I would never have stolen anything.

n) I would never have known what to do.

o) I would never have been so foolish.

p) I wouldn't have been so determined.

5.11.1

a) If you hadn't woke me up on time I would be late for work right now.

b) If I had won the lottery I would be sitting on a beach drinking margaritas right now.

c) If Tessa hadn't invited me to her French class years ago I wouldn't be fluent now.

d) If my mum and dad hadn't met I wouldn't be here right now.

e) If she hadn't been such a rude person we might be friends right now.

f) If you had studied more you could be a doctor now.

g) If he had paid the rent regularly he would still be living here.

h) If the police hadn't interviewed the witness the criminal might still be free.

i) If I had read the recipe more carefully our dinner wouldn't be in the rubbish.

j) If you had been more intelligent you wouldn't be in this trouble now.

k) If we hadn't talked clearly about how we felt we might still have a misunderstanding.

l) If Evelyn hadn't seen that advertisement in the newspaper she wouldn't be working here.

m) If I hadn't gone to the shops last night we wouldn't have any food in the house.

n) If you had walked the dog when you were supposed to you wouldn't be cleaning up a mess right now.

o) If you hadn't been such a disagreeable jerk you might have a few friends now.

Tagish Moon Publishing

Thank you for purchasing **Natural English: The Conditionals Workbook.**

Other books by Karolyn Close

➤ Natural English for Italians: 150 of the most common mistakes made by Italian speakers of English (English version)   (ISBN-13: 978-1500264765)

Natural English for Italians contains over 150 exercises which clearly explain the most common errors made by Italian speakers of English. More than a grammar book, this is one of the only resources written specifically for Italian learners of English which helps students to improve their writing and speaking by clearly explaining the difference between what seems natural and what actually works in English.

➤ Natural English For Italians: i 150 errori più comuni fatti dagli italiani che parlano inglese   (ISBN-13: 978-1505436112)

Non hai bisogno dell'ennesimo libro di grammatica!
Finalmente un libro che spiega che le frasi "I'm sorry for my late", "it depends of" e "a friend of us" sono sbagliate! Con "Natural English for Italians" potrai migliorare il tuo inglese, correggendo oltre 150 degli errori più comuni fatti dagli italiani che traducono direttamente dalla loro lingua. Scritto ad un livello B2, "Natural English for Italians" potrà essere utilizzato anche da chi ha un livello di inglese non avanzato.

➤ Natural English: The "Get" Workbook (English Edition)

(ISBN-13: 978-1502399540)

Get is one of the most flexible and commonly used words in the English language and one which can cause a lot of frustration for EFL students. It can mean buy, become, receive, understand etc. as well as being used in dozens of phrasal verbs and everyday expressions. Natural English: The "Get" Workbook has over ninety different exercises which clearly explain the uses of the word get and helps students learn English as it's really spoken.
Get ready! Get started! Get on with it! Get comfortable! Get through this book and you'll be ready for get!

➤ Bad English: A Learner's Guide to Swearing, Obscenity and Profanity

(ISBN-13: 978-1537617299)

Bad English: A Learner's Guide to Swearing, Obscenity and Profanity teaches you all the words you won't learn in your English class. A realistic look at any language tells us that there is a significant difference between the things we should say and the things we do say. When learning another language, people often want to learn all the words they're not supposed to say to their grandmothers. One of the problems of using swears / profanity / vulgarity in another language is that it might be difficult to understand just how offensive a word actually is to a native speaker. The goal of this book is to teach you not only the grammar and syntax of swearing, but to give you an idea just how vulgar or offensive a word actually is and how and when to use it (or avoid using it) before you find yourself being chased up the street by a crowd of angry people. In short, Bad English has everything you need to defend yourself verbally or get a black eye in a bar fight. Just don't practice your new skills on your grandmother.

> ## What Color Is My Happy? (ISBN-13: 978-0987767721)

What Color Is My Happy helps your children identify and talk about their emotions. By connecting feelings to smells, sounds, colors and physical sensations, you can help your child on the path toward empathy and emotional awareness. Delightfully illustrated, What Color Is My Happy opens a dialogue between parents and children about how to understand what we are feeling when we feel it. How can we express anger? What can we do when we feel frustrated? How can we show people we feel joyful or afraid? Embark on a journey of emotional awareness and empathy with your child, one that answers the question, what color is your happy?

> ## Che colore ha la felicità? (ISBN-13: 978-1492173397)

Lo scopo di Che colore ha la felicità? è aiutare i bambini a riconoscere ed esprimere le proprie emozioni. Associando gli stati d'animo a odori, suoni, colori e sensazioni fisiche, potrete infatti aiutare i vostri bambini a raggiungere una maggiore empatia e una maggiore consapevolezza emotiva. Grazie a una serie di piacevoli illustrazioni, Che colore ha la felicità? può essere uno strumento utile per i genitori perché i bambini, con l'aiuto dei loro genitori, imparino a riconoscere le emozioni che provano nel momento stesso in cui le provano. In che modo possiamo esprimere la nostra rabbia? Cosa possiamo fare quando ci sentiamo frustrati? Come possiamo far vedere agli altri che siamo allegri, oppure spaventati?
Seguite il protagonista di questo libro in un cammino di empatia e consapevolezza emotiva, rispondendo alla domanda: che colore ha la felicità secondo te?

> ## Dear Mr. Coupland (ISBN-13: 978-0987767738)

Dear Mr. Coupland,
One minute your life is right where you left it, like your keys or your glasses. The next, there's an explosion and you're standing there looking at thousands of tiny pieces of your life in a pile all around you. There's a moment of blank space where you think nothing, nothing at all, and then suddenly a horrible, sickening thought comes to you - this can't be fixed. It's like shattering your granny's favourite vase or realising too late you left your wallet on the subway. The life you had, the one you liked or hated or took for granted, it's gone and it's not coming back and now you have to go out and find a new one.
What happened to me isn't anything that doesn't happen to thousands of people, every day. I remind myself of that but to be honest, it doesn't always help.

****

When Mishka's life falls apart she retreats to her family's home on the Adriatic where she starts writing letters telling the strange story of her marriage to famed writer Douglas Coupland. In turns funny, honest and sad, Mishka slowly comes to terms with her situation while contemplating the absurdities of life and what it is to start again.

Printed in Great Britain
by Amazon

36587623R00073